The CROSS STITCH Project Book

The CROSS STITCH Project Book

Dorothea Hall

PREMIER
EDITIONS

First published 1993 by Premier Editions
An Imprint of Merehurst Limited
Ferry House, 51-57 Lacy Road, Putney, London SW15 1PR
© Copyright 1992 Merehurst Limited
ISBN 1 897730 30 6
This revised edition published 1994

Reprinted in 1996

A catalogue record for this book is available from the British Library.

Edited by Diana Brinton
Designed by Maggie Aldred
Photography by Jon Bouchier (cover, pp 10-11, 40-41, 86-87, 116-17);
all other photography by Di Lewis
Illustrations by John Hutchinson
Typesetting by BMD Graphics, Hemel Hempstead
Colour separation by Fotographics Limited, UK – Hong Kong
Printed in China by Leefung-Asco

CONTENTS

INTRODUCTION

The immense popularity of cross stitch embroidery, with its distinctive range of decorative effects, can be seen in the growing interest in hand-embroidered items for the home. These also make wonderful gifts for family and friends. The collection in this book contains something for everyone – samplers, greetings cards, cushions, pincushions and an elegant dressing-table set, as well as pretty designs for pictures and table linen. There is also an entire chapter devoted to gifts for children and babies.

Cross stitch is a wonderfully easy stitch to learn and you do not require years of experience to produce very pleasing results. Each design is carefully charted and colour coded and has accompanying step-by-step instructions for making up the item.

While some designs are very easy and quite suitable for beginners, others are a little more challenging and may involve working with many colours. Handling them can seem daunting at first, but your skill will very quickly improve with practice.

Learning to work with several needles threaded with different colours is useful, and you will avoid having to start and finish new threads with each colour area.

There is also a Basic Skills section, which covers everything from preparing and stretching your fabric in an embroidery frame to mounting your cross stitch ready for display.

All the necessary skills are simply explained, thus ensuring that, whatever your experience, you will be able to enjoy creating beautiful things for the home.

BASIC SKILLS

BEFORE YOU BEGIN

PREPARING THE FABRIC
Even with an average amount of handling, many evenweave fabrics tend to fray at the edges, so it is a good idea to overcast the raw edges, using ordinary sewing thread, before you begin.

THE INSTRUCTIONS
Each project begins with a full list of the materials that you will require; Aida, Tula, Lugana and Linda are all fabrics produced by Zweigart. Note that the measurements given for the embroidery fabric include a minimum of 3cm (1¼in) all around to allow for stretching it in a frame and preparing the edges to prevent them from fraying.

A colour key for DMC stranded embroidery cotton is given with each chart. It is assumed that you will need to buy one skein of each colour mentioned, even though you may use less, but where two or more skeins are needed, this information is included in the main list of requirements.

Should you wish to use Anchor or Madeira stranded embroidery cottons, refer to the conversion chart given at the back of the book (page 159).

To work from the charts, particularly those where several symbols are used in close proximity, some readers may find it helpful to have the chart enlarged so that the squares and symbols can be seen more easily. Many photocopying services will do this for a minimum charge.

Before you begin to embroider, always mark the centre of the design with two lines of basting stitches, one vertical and one horizontal, running from edge to edge of the fabric, as indicated by the arrows on the charts.

As you stitch, use the centre lines given on the chart and the basting threads on your fabric as reference points for counting the squares and threads to position your design accurately.

WORKING IN A HOOP
A hoop is the most popular frame for use with small areas of embroidery. It consists of two rings, one fitted inside the other; the outer ring usually has an

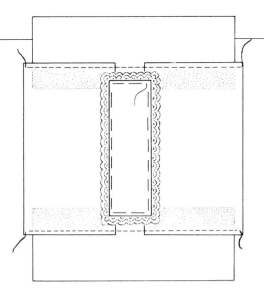

adjustable screw attachment so that it can be tightened to hold the stretched fabric in place. Hoops are available in several sizes, ranging from 10cm (4in) in diameter to quilting hoops with a diameter of 38cm (15in). Hoops with table stands or floor stands attached are also available.

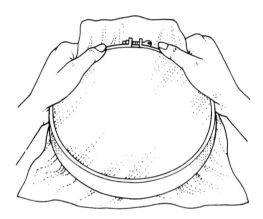

1 To stretch your fabric in a hoop, place the area to be embroidered over the inner ring and press the outer ring over it with the tension screw released. Tissue paper can be placed between the outer ring and the embroidery, so that the hoop does not mark the fabric. Lay the tissue paper over the fabric when you set it in the hoop, then tear away the central, embroidery area.

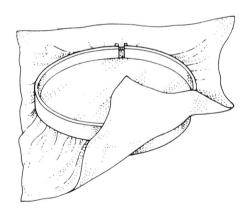

2 Smooth the fabric and, if needed, straighten the grain before tightening the screw. The fabric should be evenly stretched.

EXTENDING EMBROIDERY FABRIC

It is easy to extend a piece of embroidery fabric, such as a bookmark, to stretch it in a hoop.

● Fabric oddments of a similar weight can be used. Simply cut four pieces to size (in other words, to the measurement that will fit both the embroidery fabric and your hoop) and baste them to each side

of the embroidery fabric before stretching it in the hoop in the usual way.

WORKING IN A RECTANGULAR FRAME

Rectangular frames are more suitable for larger pieces of embroidery. They consist of two rollers, with tapes attached, and two flat side pieces, which slot into the rollers and are held in place by pegs or screw attachments. Available in different sizes, either alone or with adjustable table or floor stands, frames are measured by the length of the roller tape, and range in size from 30cm (12in) to 68cm (27in).

As alternatives to a slate frame, canvas stretchers and the backs of old picture frames can be used. Provided there is sufficient extra fabric around the finished size of the embroidery, the edges can be turned under and simply attached with drawing pins (thumb tacks) or staples.

1 To stretch your fabric in a rectangular frame, cut out the fabric, allowing at least an extra 5cm (2in) all around the finished size of the embroidery. Baste a single 12mm (½in) turning on the top and bottom edges and oversew strong tape, 2.5cm (1in) wide, to the other two sides. Mark the centre line both ways with basting stitches. Working from the centre outwards and using strong thread, oversew the top and bottom edges to the roller tapes. Fit the side pieces into the slots, and roll any extra fabric on one roller until the fabric is taut.

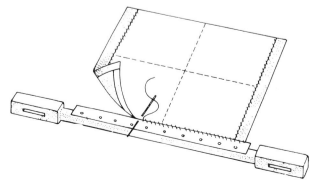

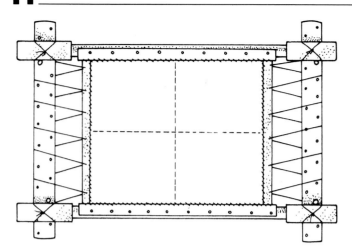

2 Insert the pegs or adjust the screw attachments to secure the frame. Thread a large-eyed needle (chenille needle) with strong thread or fine string and lace both edges, securing the ends around the intersections of the frame. Lace the webbing at 2.5cm (1in) intervals, stretching the fabric evenly.

ENLARGING A GRAPH PATTERN

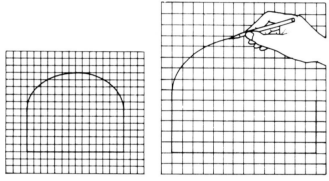

● To enlarge a graph pattern, you will need a sheet of graph paper ruled in 1cm (⅜in) squares, a ruler and pencil. If, for example, the scale is one square to 5cm (2in) you should first mark the appropriate lines to give a grid of the correct size. Copy the graph freehand from the small grid to the larger one, completing one square at a time. Use a ruler to draw the straight lines first, and then copy the freehand curves.

TO BIND AN EDGE

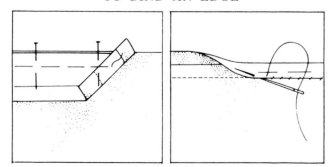

1 Open out the turning on one edge of the bias binding and pin in position on the right side of the fabric, matching the fold to the seamline. Fold over the cut end of the binding. Finish by overlapping the starting point by about 12mm (½in). Baste and machine stitch along the seamline.
2 Fold the binding over the raw edge to the wrong side, baste and, using matching sewing thread, neatly hem to finish.

PIPED SEAMS

Contrasting piping adds a special decorative finish to a seam and looks particularly attractive on items such as cushions and cosies.

You can cover piping cord with either bias-cut fabric of your choice or a bias binding; alternatively, ready-covered piping cord is available in several widths and many colours.

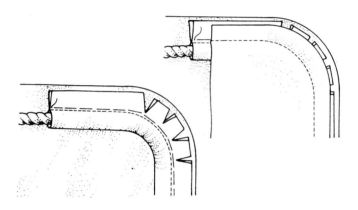

1 To apply piping, pin and baste it to the right side of the fabric, with seam lines matching. Clip into the seam allowance where necessary.
2 With right sides together, place the second piece of fabric on top, enclosing the piping. Baste and then either hand stitch in place or machine stitch, using a zipper foot. Stitch as close to the piping as possible, covering the first line of stitching.

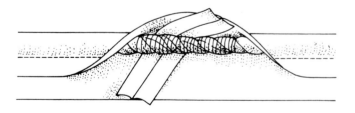

3 To join ends of piping cord together, first overlap the two ends by about 2.5cm (1in). Unpick the two cut ends of bias to reveal the cord. Join the bias strip as shown. Trim and press the seam open. Unravel and splice the two ends of the cord. Fold the bias strip over it, and finish basting around the edge.

MOUNTING EMBROIDERY

The cardboard should be cut to the size of the finished embroidery, with an extra 6mm (¼in) added all around to allow for the recess in the frame.

LIGHTWEIGHT FABRICS

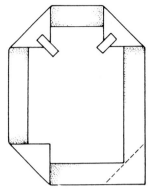
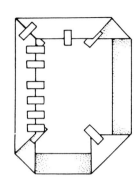

1 Place the emboidery face down, with the cardboard centred on top, and basting and pencil lines matching. Begin by folding over the fabric at each corner and securing it with masking tape.
2 Working first on one side and then the other, fold over the fabric on all sides and secure it firmly with pieces of masking tape, placed about 2.5cm (1in) apart. Also neaten the mitred corners with masking tape, pulling the fabric tightly to give a firm, smooth finish.

HEAVIER FABRICS

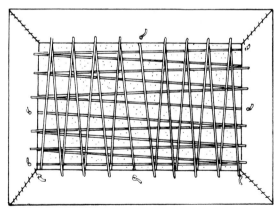

● Lay the embroidery face down, with the cardboard centred on top; fold over the edges of the fabric on opposite sides, making mitred folds at the corners, and lace across, using strong thread. Repeat on the other two sides. Finally, pull up the stitches fairly tightly to stretch the fabric firmly over the cardboard. Overstitch the mitred corners.

CROSS STITCH

For all cross stitch embroidery, the following two methods of working are used. In each case, neat rows of vertical stitches are produced on the back of the fabric.

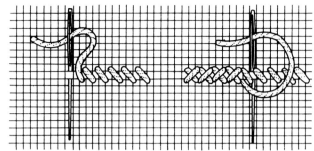

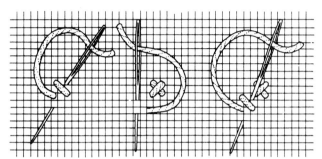

● When stitching large areas, work in horizontal rows. Working from right to left, complete the first row of evenly spaced diagonal stitches over the number of threads specified in the project instructions. Then, working from left to right, repeat the process. Continue in this way, making sure each stitch crosses in the same direction.
● When stitching diagonal lines, work downwards, completing each stitch before moving to the next.

BACKSTITCH

Backstitch is used in the projects to give emphasis to a particular foldline, an outline or a shadow. The stitches are worked over the same number of threads as the cross stitch, forming continuous straight or diagonal lines.

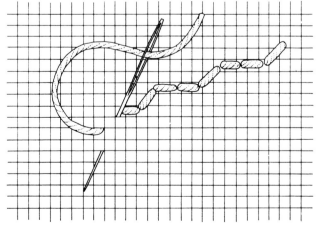

● Make the first stitch from left to right; pass the needle behind the fabric, and bring it out one stitch length ahead to the left. Repeat and continue in this way along the line.

ACCESSORIES
for the
HOME

*The projects in this chapter have
been selected to enhance every room
in the house. Pretty cushions, a
tea-cosy, a sampler and a table
runner are included here – they all
make ideal gifts or charming
additions to your home.*

House and Garden Sampler

Country accents abound in this sampler in the traditional style, based on the house-and-garden theme. To personalize the design, you could, with a little judicious pre-planning, depict your own house, add your initials (and the date) and, using the alphabet in the sampler design, even add a motto or dedication.

HOUSE AND GARDEN SAMPLER

YOU WILL NEED

For a Sampler measuring 23cm (9in) square (unframed):

35cm (14in) square of white linen, 26 threads to 2.5cm (1in)
DMC stranded embroidery cotton in the colours given in the panel
23cm (9in) square of 3mm (1/8in) cardboard for mounting the embroidery
23cm (9in) square of lightweight synthetic batting
Strong thread for securing the mounted fabric
Picture frame of your choice
No26 tapestry needle

•

Following the alphabet given with the sampler, select your chosen initials and, using a soft pencil, draw them on the chart. For three initials, ignore the centre diamond and experiment with the spacing, positioning them within the central area. You may prefer to add the date of the embroidery, or a longer dedication. In which case, ignore the two hearts and the two outer diamonds and use the whole of the lower area. You will find it easier to follow if this is charted on a separate piece of graph paper, matching the grid to that given in the book. If you do remove the hearts, it would be nice to work the embroidery in red, or perhaps the blue, from the border. Whichever colour you use, it will be helpful to chart your wording as a guide before working the embroidery.

THE EMBROIDERY

With the prepared fabric stretched in a frame (see page 7) and the centre lines basted both ways, begin the embroidery. Using two strands of thread in the needle and carefully following the chart, complete the embroidery, working one cross stitch over two threads of fabric. Remember that with very openweave fabrics it is important not to strand the thread from one area to another, otherwise it will show through on the right side. Begin and finish threads underneath an embroidered area, and trim all loose ends when finishing.

Remove the finished embroidery from the frame, but do not take out the basting threads at this stage. Steam press on the wrong side.

FRAMING THE SAMPLER

A thin layer of batting is placed between the cardboard and the embroidery. In this case it helps to give an opaque quality to the openweave linen. To centre the cardboard over the embroidery, first mark the centre line of the cardboard both ways, using a soft pencil. Similarly, mark the batting by placing a pin at the central point on each side.

Lay the embroidery face down; centre the batting on top, and then the cardboard, with basting, pins and pencil lines matching.

Working on one side and then the opposite side, fold over the edges of the fabric on all sides and secure with masking tape (see page 9) first removing the pins. Neaten the corners by folding them in to form a mitre and secure with masking tape. Remove the basting threads.

Insert the glass and mounted embroidery into your picture frame; add the backing board provided, and secure with picture tacks. Cover the tacks with broad sticky tape to neaten.

HOUSE AND GARDEN ▶

=		ecru	✚	351	salmon pink
◺		pale yellow	•	350	brick red
◣	677	naples yellow	S	927	pale blue
↑	743	soft yellow	○	597	blue
◆	972	deep gold	△	523	pale green
I	352	pale salmon pink (and bks window sashes)	⊡	732	olive
			↓	3012	khaki

A Child's Picture

Every picture tells a story, and this embroidery, the Little Disaster, stitched in minute detail, tells of a doting farmer and his luckless pony-ride in true pictorial style.

This elaborate picture, which uses some 26 different colours of embroidery cotton, will prove an enjoyable challenge to the more experienced cross-stitch embroiderer, and when you have finished you may well feel that it is worthy of a place in your hall or living room rather than a child's bedroom.

T white

H 745 pale yellow
  (and bks 742*)

S 677 pale gold
  (and bks 729*)

÷ 722 orange

△ 783 ochre

◓ 951 flesh
  (and bks 758*)

I 435 rust
  (and bks 300*)

◇ 519 blue

↑ 472 pale green

◺ 469 sap green
  (and bks 935*)

↓ 503 blue green
  (and bks 500*)

‖ 3345 dark green

✕ 712 cream
  (and bks 842*)

◣ 822 beige (bks 640)

✳ 3045 light brown
  (bks 435)

  839 dark brown
  (bks 435)

◆ 3072 pale grey

○ 926 blue grey
  (and bks 311*)

● 310 black (bks 712)

*Note: 8 additional
backstitch colours**

A CHILD'S PICTURE

YOU WILL NEED

For an unframed picture measuring
23cm (9in) square:

35cm (14in) square of blue evenweave (Aida)
fabric, 18 threads to 2.5cm (1in)
23cm (9in) square of lightweight batting
DMC stranded embroidery cotton in the colours
given in the panel
No26 tapestry needle
23cm (9in) square of 3mm (⅛in) cardboard
Masking tape for securing the mounted fabric
Picture frame of your choice

•

THE EMBROIDERY

Referring to the instructions on page 7, stretch
the prepared fabric in a frame. Using two strands
of thread in the needle and carefully following the
chart, begin the embroidery. Work the outline and
the two horizontal dividing lines first, making sure
you count the correct number of threads between.

Finish the cross stitching and, using a single
strand of thread, work the backstitching to complete the embroidery.

Remove the embroidery from the frame and, if
necessary, steam press on the wrong side.

FRAMING THE PICTURE

To offset the embroidery, the picture here includes
a border of background fabric 2cm (¾in) wide,
which you can easily adjust to suit your own prefer-
ence. You may wish, for example, to add a
decorative outer border of your own devising,
embroidered in cross stitching. Also, to give the
finished picture a slightly padded look, a layer of
lightweight batting is inserted between the fabric
and mounting card.

Mount the picture, following the instructions
given for the heavier fabrics on page 9 before
finally inserting it into the picture frame.

Of Princes and Princesses

Traditional tales of adventure and of love lost and gained have been captured in this delightful set of scatter cushions, which would look charming mixed with lacy pillows.

OF PRINCES
AND PRINCESSES

YOU WILL NEED

For three cushion covers, each measuring
27.5cm (11in) square:

*35cm (14in) square each of apple green,
pink and cream evenweave Aida fabric,
14 threads to 2.5cm (1in)
30cm (12in) square each of matching or contrast
backing fabric
DMC stranded emboidery cotton in the colours
given in the appropriate panel
3 × 30cm (12in) square cushion pads
28 white seed pearls for the Swineherd design
No24 tapestry needle and No9 crewel needle
Matching sewing threads*

•

THE EMBROIDERY

All three cushions are made in the following way.
For one cushion, stretch the prepared fabric in a
frame (see page 7) and baste the centre lines in
both directions.

Using two strands of thread in the needle, and
following the appropriate chart, complete the cross
stitching. Also work the backstitching with two
strands of thread in the needle, with the exception
of the following details which are worked with a
single strand: Beauty and the Beast – the beast's
teeth and tusks; Sleeping Beauty – Beauty's face
and hands and her dress, and the prince's face. The
pearls around the Swineherd design are sewn on
with matching sewing thread and a fine crewel
needle.

Complete the embroidery by backstitching the
outline around the design, using two strands of
thread in the needle. Remove the finished embroidery from the frame and steam press on the wrong
side. Do not over press the pearls.

MAKING UP THE CUSHION

Using the basting threads as a guide, trim the edges
of the embroidery symmetrically to measure 30cm
(12in) square. Place the backing fabric and the
embroidery right sides together, baste and machine
stitch around the edges, taking a 12mm (½in)
seam, and leaving a 20cm (8in) opening in the
middle of one side.

Trim across the corners and turn the cover
through to the right side. Insert the cushion pad
and, using matching sewing thread, slipstitch the
opening to close.

Attach a small tassel to each corner of the border.
To make a tassel, wind matching embroidery thread
(six strands) five or six times around a narrow piece
of card, about 2cm (¾in) wide. Thread a needle
with a short length of thread (two strands), slip the
threads off the card and wind the thread several
times around, close to the top, making the normal
tassel shape. Pass the needle through the loops at
the top and repeat a second time. Pull the thread
firmly and bring the needle up through the centre,
ready to sew the tassel in place.

Cut through the loops at the bottom of the tassel;
fan out the threads, and trim across. Neatly stitch
a tassel to each corner, as shown in the photograph.

STITCHING ON BEADS

Use the same method to attach small, even-shaped
beads and pearls.

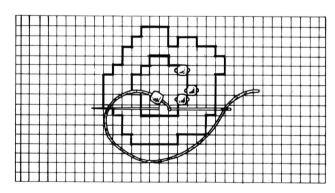

• Using either a fine crewel needle, number 9 or
10, or a beading straw for very fine beads, and
sewing thread or fine silk, bring out the needle and
thread on a bead. Reinsert the needle through the
same hole, then make a stitch the width of the bead
(and in this case, the width of the cross stitch), and
pull through, with the thread below the needle.
Repeat, completing the design as instructed.

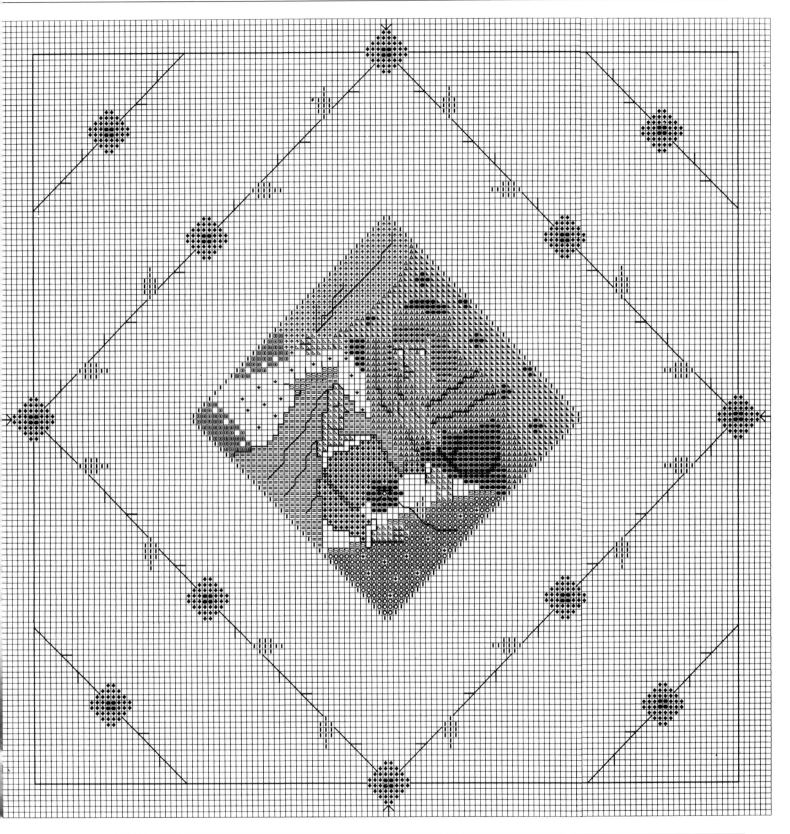

SLEEPING BEAUTY ▲

□ white

= 3078 pale yellow (bks 743)

○ 743 yellow

S 733 gold (bks on
    Beauty's face and

hands, and outer
lines on hair)

↓ gold thread

◁ 754 flesh (bks 732 for
    prince)

● 351 red (bks around

Beauty's dress and
the mouths of both
figures)

◆ 747 pale blue

△ 924 dark blue (bks 504)

↑ 504 pale green

| 581 green (ground
    pattern and thorns)

✳ 732 deep olive (bks on
    prince's face)

◤ 644 fawn

⊡ 613 light brown

SLEEPING BEAUTY

Coming to the rescue of the stricken parents, the last fairy announced that although she could not completely destroy the curse, she could soften its effect:
'Rose will prick her finger, but she will not die. Instead she and all within the palace will fall asleep until one day a prince's kiss will wake her.'

THE SWINEHERD

In exchange for one hundred kisses the swineherd agrees to give the princess his pretty little pipkin, with tinkling bells that make the sweetest music, which has completely won the heart of the greedy princess.

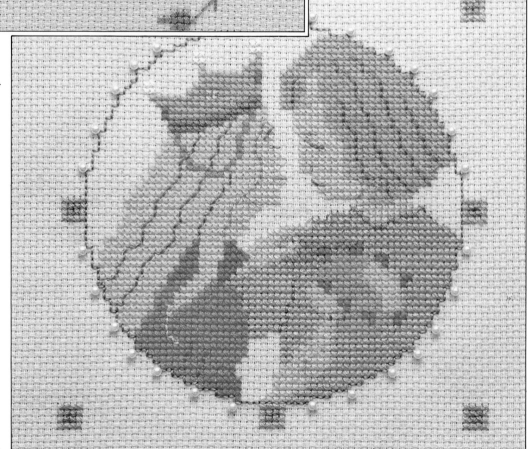

BEAUTY AND THE BEAST

Remembering her dream, Beauty flew to the
garden where she found poor Beast stretched
out, quite senseless, as though dead. 'Beast,
oh Beast,' she wept, lifting his huge head onto
her lap. 'You must not die, I love you.'

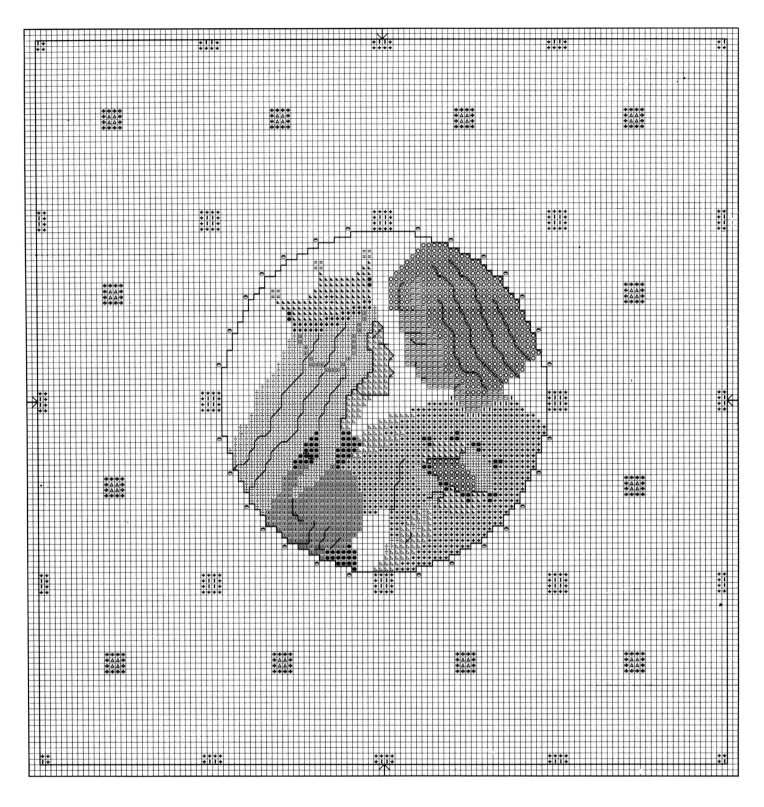

THE SWINEHERD ▲

= white

◒ white seed pearls

○ 834 pale gold (bks 680)

÷ 744 yellow (bks 680)

◆ 680 gold (princess' eyebrows)

◣ 725 deep yellow (bks hair line next to princess' face)

⊆ 3779 flesh (bks 680)

△ 963 pale pink (bks 605; bks princess' eye 959)

✱ 605 sugar pink

⊡ 3706 peach pink (bks 603)

● 603 deep pink

△ 3609 dull pink

↓ 959 veridian green (bks 3364)

| 3364 green (bks circle outline and the square outlining the design)

BEAUTY AND THE BEAST ▼

- □ white
- ÷ 727 pale yellow (bks on shawl and dress cuff)
- ◣ 3046 pale gold (bks on dress)
- ◤ 783 yellow
- ↑ 948 flesh (bks 224)
- Ɩ 3713 pale pink
- ✱ 224 dusky pink
- △ 352 pink
- ● 3705 red (bks on snout; bks 731)
- ◆ 680 ginger (bks around feather)
- = 747 pale blue
- S 3053 sage green
- ⊡ 731 dark olive
- ↓ 3051 very dark olive
- ○ 3045 light brown (bks 731)

27

Snowflakes

This charming yet easy-to-make table runner, embroidered in a single colour and in a relatively large stitch, features a series of snowflakes. The edges are hemstitched in a matching colour and simply fringed. A runner as delightful as this can be used throughout the Christmas period and then put away, to be brought out again in successive years to add to the festive atmosphere.

SNOWFLAKES

YOU WILL NEED

For a Table runner measuring 65cm × 46cm (25½in × 18in):

65cm × 46cm (25½in × 18in) of cream huckaback, 10 threads (blocks) to 2.5cm (1in); an alternative fabric such as Zweigart's Tula can be used
3 skeins of red 326 DMC stranded embroidery cotton and 1 skein of ecru for the hemstitching
No18 tapestry needle

•

To fringe the edges, first press the fabric and trim the edges along the straight grain. Using two strands of ecru thread in the needle, hemstitch around the edges, as shown, placing the stitching seven blocks in from the raw edge. Make each hem stitch two blocks across by one block deep. Leave the fringing until the embroidery is finished.

THE EMBROIDERY

Baste the centre of the fabric both ways and then baste a central rectangle, as shown on the chart, to give the positioning lines for the four smaller motifs and spots. The rectangle should measure 140 stitches (blocks) across by 80 stitches deep.

Referring to the positioning diagram and chart, complete the cross stitching, using three strands of thread in the needle throughout. Work each motif with the fabric stretched in a hoop (see page 6). Remove the basting threads and steam press the runner on the wrong side, if needed. Remove the fringing threads.

FULL-LENGTH TABLE RUNNER

For a full-length table runner, first measure the length of your table. If you would prefer it to over-hang at the sides, add an extra 20cm (8in) at each end. Decide on an appropriate width, not usually more than half the width of your table, and cut out the fabric. Baste the positioning lines and hem-stitch the edges, following the instructions above.

Similarly, embroider the motifs beginning in the centre of the runner. Repeat further snowflakes, in pattern sequence, to fill the two sides, placing a large snowflake next to the two smaller ones, and so on.

PLACEMATS AND COASTERS

Instead of a table runner, you may wish to make individual placemats and/or coasters.

For a placemat, measuring about 26cm × 36cm (10in × 14in), embroider a large snowflake in the centre, and for a coaster, measuring about 12cm (4½in) square, embroider a smaller snowflake in the middle. Hemstitch the edges as for the runner, and fringe to complete.

HEMSTITCH

This stitch is the traditional way of finishing the hems of embroidered napkins and tablecloths. For a fringed hem, remove a single thread at the hem and stitch along the line as shown. When you have finished, remove the weft threads below the hem-stitching, to make the fringe.

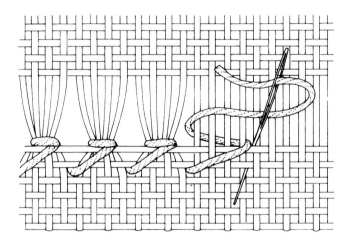

• Bring the needle out on the right side, two threads below the drawn-thread line. Working from left to right, pick up either two or three threads, as shown in the diagram. Bring the needle out again and insert it behind the fabric, to emerge two threads down, ready to make the next stitch. Before reinserting the needle, pull the thread tight, so that the bound threads form a neat group.

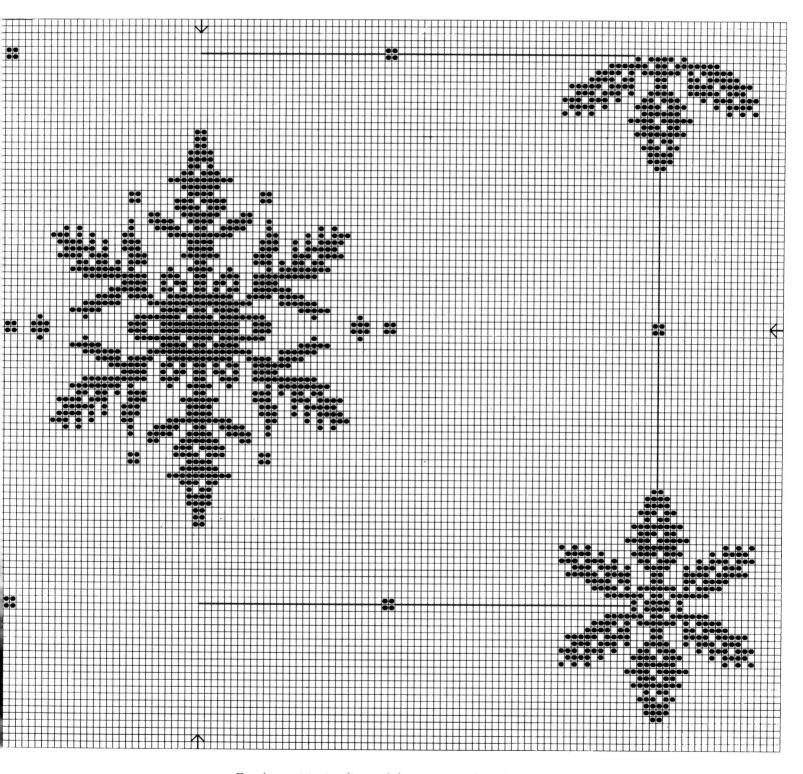

SNOWFLAKES ▼

● 326 red

For the positioning lines of the outer motifs and spots,
complete the rectangle, reversing from the centre lines.

TEA-COSY

YOU WILL NEED

For a tea-cosy measuring 37cm × 27cm
(14½in × 10½in):

*90cm × 30cm (36in × 12in) of blue evenweave
Lugana, 26 threads to 2.5 cm (1in)
90cm × 60cm (36in × 24in) of pale blue lawn
for the lining
76cm × 30cm (30in × 12in) of medium-weight
synthetic batting
150cm (60in) of red bias binding, 2.5cm (1in) wide
DMC stranded embroidery cotton in the colours
given in the panel on page 35
No24 tapestry needle
Matching sewing threads
Tracing paper*

●

THE EMBROIDERY

Cut the evenweave fabric in half to give two pieces,
each measuring 45cm × 30cm (18in × 12in). With
the edges of one section prepared and stretched
in a hoop, baste the positioning lines for the
embroidery, as shown on the chart.

Complete the embroidery, using two strands of
thread throughout, except for the outlines around
both faces and hands, where a single thread is
used. Steam press the finished embroidery on the
wrong side.

MAKING UP THE TEA-COSY

To make the paper pattern for the cosy, first enlarge
the graph pattern given opposite on tracing paper
(see page 8), and cut out. Seam allowances of
12mm (½in) all around are included.

Place the pattern on the evenweave fabric with
straight grain and centre lines matching, and cut
out. In the same way, cut out the lining and the
batting as instructed.

To facilitate laundering, the outer cover of the
cosy is detachable from the lining and is simply
bound around the edges with bias binding.

For the loop, cut 8cm (3in) of contrast bias binding and machine stitch the long edges together.

Fold in half to form a loop. Baste to the centre top
of the front section, laying it on the right side of
the fabric, raw edges placed just inside the seam
allowance.

With right sides outside, place both sections of
the cosy together and baste around the curved edge.
Pin and baste the double-folded bias binding
around the curved edge and machine stitch, using
matching sewing thread. Trim the binding level
with the lower edge. Bind the lower edge in the
same way, overlapping the cut ends by 12mm
(½in). Cut the end with the grain of the bias and
fold under 6mm (¼in) to neaten. Remove all
basting stitches and press the finished cover.

THE LINING

Place the four lining sections in two pairs, each
with right sides together, and baste and stitch the
bottom edges, taking 12mm (½in) seams. Press the
seams and turn each section right side out.

Cut 12mm (½in) from the bottom edge of each
batting section, and pin a batting section into each
lining pocket. Baste along the curved seamline,
then place the two lining sections together and
machine zigzag along the curved seam. Trim the
excess fabric, close to the stitching, and slip the
lining inside the cover to complete the tea-cosy.

TEA-COSY

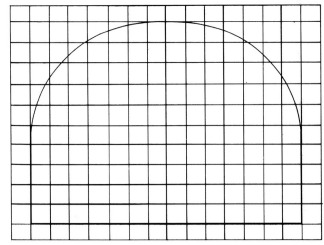

1 SQUARE = 2.5cm (1in)
Cut two from evenweave
Cut two from batting
Cut four from lining

Tea-Cosy

Embroidered in bright, cheery colours, this large, padded cosy will keep your tea steaming hot right to the last cup.

If you prefer to make a cosy for a coffee pot, it would be an easy matter to make the sides narrower and continue the simple, cloudy outlines of the tree upward to fill the required space. It might also be a good idea to add a few more leaves and more depth to the bottom of the design, to keep the proportions correct.

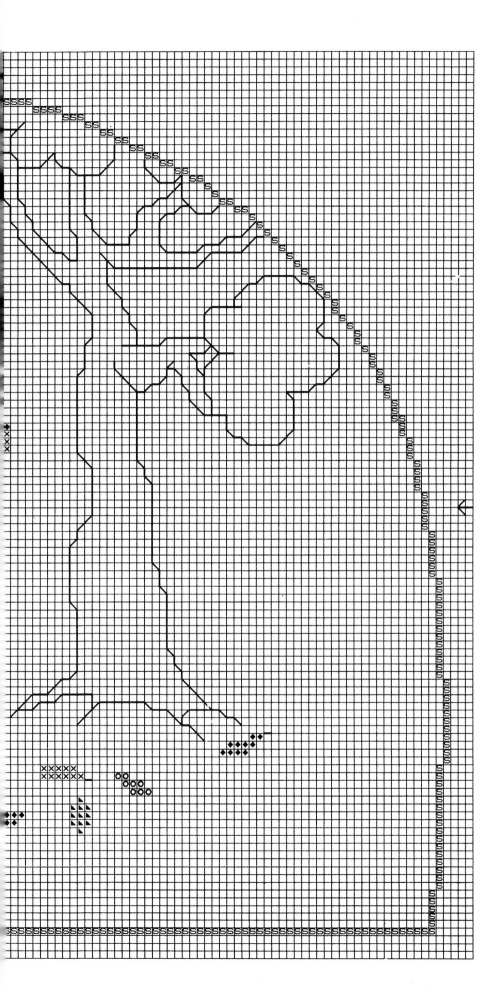

◄ HANSEL AND GRETEL

◇ white (bks 799)

✕ 743 pale yellow (bks 833)

= 972 yellow

○ 833 deep gold (bks on right
tree – second to top cluster
of leaves; left tree – second
to bottom cluster of leaves)

÷ 951 flesh (bks 869)

✱ 224 pink

I 223 rose pink

◆ 976 ginger (bks on right tree –
top and bottom clusters of
leaves; left tree – second to
top and bottom clusters
of leaves)

● 900 red (bks on right tree –
smallest cluster of leaves;
left tree – top cluster
of leaves)

S 732 green

◣ 733 olive green (bks tree
trunks and branches)

⊖ 747 pale turquoise

‖ 597 turquoise (bks 733)

◹ 799 blue

✦ 3750 dark blue (bks 799)

⊡ 3799 very dark blue

△ 869 brown
(bks bird's eye and legs)

Four Seasons Placemat

This delightful placemat, with its four seasons design, featuring cherries, strawberries, rosehips and cranberries, has a prettily scalloped border, edged with contrast cotton binding.

A single placemat makes a cheerful accessory when eating alone, or it could double as a traycloth. You could also make one for each member of the family, perhaps embroidering just a single motif on each one, placing it at the centre top, to reduce the amount of embroidery involved.

FOUR SEASONS PLACEMAT

YOU WILL NEED

For a Placemat measuring 39cm × 29cm
(15½in × 11½in):

*46cm × 35cm (18in × 14in) of white linen,
26 threads to 2.5cm (1in)
130cm (1½yd) of contrast cotton bias binding,
2.5cm (1in) wide
DMC stranded embroidery cotton in the colours
given in the panel
No26 tapestry needle
Sewing thread to match the contrast binding
20cm × 15cm (8in × 6in) of cardboard for a
template (use a breakfast cereal box or
similar packaging)
Tracing paper*

•

THE EMBROIDERY

Prepare the edges of the fabric and baste the centre
both ways. Then, following the measurements given
on the chart, baste the central rectangle, which
forms the positioning lines for each motif. The com-
pleted rectangle should measure 200 threads across
by 140 threads down.

With the fabric stretched in a hoop and following
the chart and colour keys, complete the embroidery. Use two strands of thread in the needle, and
work one cross stitch over two threads throughout.

Steam press on the wrong side. Retain the basting
stitches at this stage.

DRAWING THE SCALLOPED EDGE

Using a soft pencil, trace the quarter section of the
placemat, as shown on this page. Turn the tracing
over; place it on the cardboard, and go over the
outline to transfer it to the cardboard. Make sure
that the two straight sides meet at an exact right
angle. Cut out the template.

Lay the embroidery face down, and place the
template over one quarter, matching the straight
edges to the central basting stitches. Lightly draw
around the scalloped edge. Repeat this for the
remaining sections. Carefully cut out the placemat
and remove the basting stitches.

BINDING THE EDGE

With right sides and raw edges together, pin and
baste the binding around the edge (see page 8),
beginning in the corner of one scallop. Where the
two ends of the binding meet, overlap by 2cm
(¾in), turning the raw, overlapped end under by
6mm (¼in) to neaten it. Using matching sewing
thread, machine stitch or backstitch in place.

Bring the binding over the raw edge of the fabric
and hem, gently easing it around curves and sewing
into the back of the first stitching line to prevent
the thread from showing on the right side.

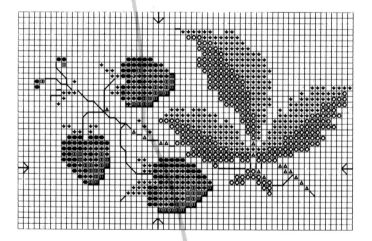

STRAWBERRIES ▲

⊡ pale pink (bks 335)
✚ 335 strawberry pink,
   plus outline around
   light side of strawberry

● 321 red
↓ 470 pale green
○ 3348 green
△ 731 olive green
   (and bks stems)

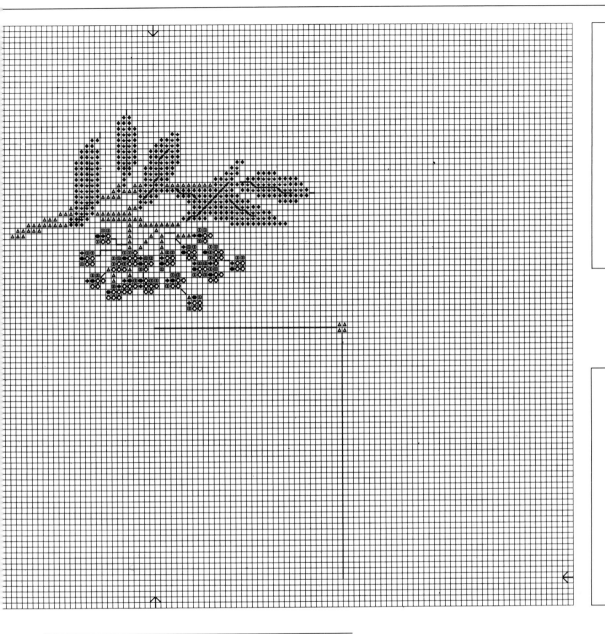

CRANBERRIES ◀

△	744	old gold (and corner spots)
●	718	magenta
○	3752	pale blue
⊡	334	blue
✳	3750	dark blue
◆	564	pale green
↓	959	green (bks 733)

ROSEHIPS ▼

○	676	yellow
●	350	red
△	976	rust
⊡	3766	blue
✳	581	sap green
↓	3012	browny green (and bks hip tips)

To complete the scalloped outline, reverse the template on the centre lines of each quarter section and draw around.

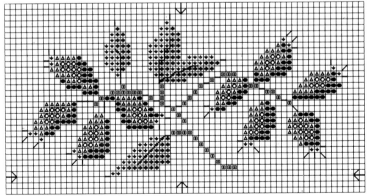

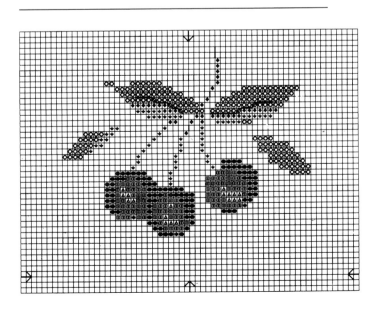

CHERRIES ◀

△	962	pale pink	○	945	pale green (bks 943)
⊡	602	pink	◆	992	sage green
●	600	red	↓	943	veridian green
✳	814	deep red			

SPECIAL OCCASIONS *and* CELEBRATIONS

Whether the occasion is an engagement, wedding, special birthday or anniversary, a cross stitch gift makes a memorable keepsake that will be treasured by the recipient for many years to come.

Celebration Cushions

A pretty cushion, embroidered to celebrate a particular occasion, always makes a very acceptable gift. Each motif – confetti-strewn wedding bells, a floral Valentine heart and a Christmas wreath of poinsettias and holly – is bordered with ribbon, bows or braid, and each cushion is finished with delicate lace trim.

CELEBRATION CUSHIONS

YOU WILL NEED

For the Wedding Anniversary cushion, measuring overall 25cm (10in) square:

Two 25cm (10in) squares of white Davosa, 18 threads to 2.5cm (1in)
DMC stranded embroidery cotton in the colours given in the appropriate panel
140cm (1½yd) of white lace trim, 2.5cm (1in) wide
Gold embroidery thread for the border
23cm (9in) square cushion pad
No26 tapestry needle
Matching sewing thread

For the Christmas Time cushion, measuring overall 25cm (10in) square:

Two 25cm (10in) squares of khaki Aida, 16 threads to 2.5cm (1in)
DMC stranded embroidery cotton in the colours given in the appropriate panel
140cm (1½yd) of deep cream lace trim, 2cm (¾in) wide
23cm (9in) square cushion pad
No24 tapestry needle
Matching sewing thread

For the Valentine cushion, measuring overall 25cm (10in) square:

Two 23cm (9in) squares of white linen, 21 threads to 2.5cm (1in)
DMC stranded embroidery cotton in the colours given in the appropriate panel
140cm (1½yd) of white lace trim, 4cm (1½in) wide
180cm (2yd) of pink parcel ribbon
20cm (8in) square cushion pad
No26 tapestry needle
Matching sewing thread

WEDDING ANNIVERSARY

Baste the centre both ways on one of the squares of fabric and stretch it in a hoop (see page 6). Following the chart and colour key, and using two strands of thread in the needle throughout, begin the embroidery, stitching the gold thread details first. On this particular fabric, it is better to work one complete cross stitch at a time, over each intersection, to prevent the threads from slipping. Finish the embroidery and then outline the base of the bells in silver thread. Steam press on the wrong side.

For the border, follow the chart and, using two strands of gold thread in the needle, embroider the double lines, stitching under one thread and over five. Make sure that the pattern of stitching is the same on each line.

MAKING UP THE CUSHION

Trim the embroidery to measure 21.5cm (8½in) square. Using a tiny french seam, join the short edges of the lace together.

Run a gathering thread close to the straight edge of the lace. Pulling up the gathers to fit, lay the lace on the right side of the embroidery, with the decorative edge facing inwards and the straight edge parallel to the edge of the fabric and just inside the seam allowance. Baste in position, adjusting the gathers to allow extra fullness at the corners. Machine stitch in place.

With the right sides together, centre the backing fabric over the embroidered fabric and lace. Trim to size, then baste and machine stitch around, leaving a 13cm (5in) opening in the middle of one side. Remove all basting stitches; trim across the seam allowance at the corners, and turn the cover right side out. Insert the cushion pad and slipstitch the opening to close it.

CHRISTMAS TIME

Following the appropriate chart, complete the embroidery as for the Wedding Anniversary cushion. In this case, however, the design is embroidered on Aida fabric, so the cross stitches can be made in two stages, if you prefer. Embroider the backstitch details last of all.

Steam press the embroidery on the wrong side.

Trim the embroidery and backing fabric 24cm (9½in) square. Add the lace edging and make up the cushion following the previous instructions.

VALENTINE

Stretch the prepared fabric in a hoop and, following the relevant chart, complete the embroidery, using two strands of thread in the needle and working one cross stitch over two threads throughout. Steam press the finished embroidery on the wrong side.

For the ribbon border, cut the parcel ribbon into four 27.5cm (11in) lengths and four 17.5cm (7in) lengths. Withdraw a single thread from the ground fabric on each side, six threads out from the embroidered motif.

Following the diagram, thread one short length of ribbon from a point where two drawn-thread lines intersect and out to the nearest edge; take the ribbon under four threads and over six, leaving a tail for tying at the intersection.

Thread a longer length from the opposite edge of the fabric to meet the first at the same intersection, again leaving a tying thread at this point. Repeat on all sides to complete the ribbon border. The bows are tied after the cushion seams have been stitched, securing the outer ends of the ribbons.

FINISHING THE CUSHION

Trim the embroidery and the backing fabric to measure 20cm (8in) square. Add the lace edging and complete the cushion, following the instructions for the Wedding Anniversary cushion.

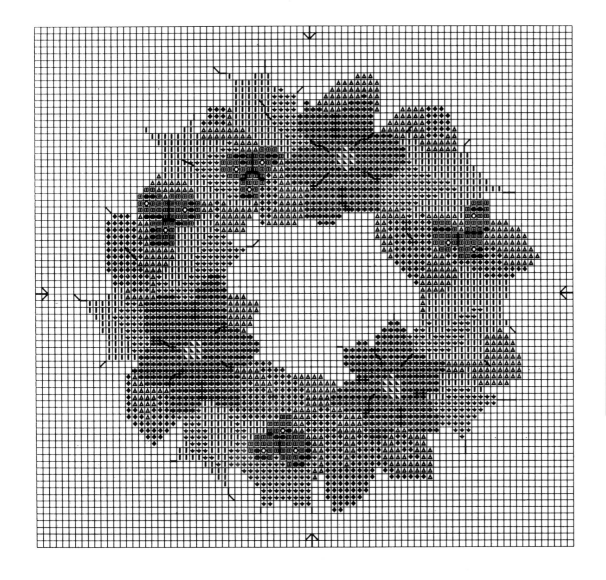

CHRISTMAS TIME ◄

◣	725	yellow
○	604	pink
⊡	600	deep pink
✳	606	red
●	915	purple (and bks poinsettia)
◆	772	pale yellow green
△	907	yellow green
I	955	pale green (bks 912)
↓	912	veridian green

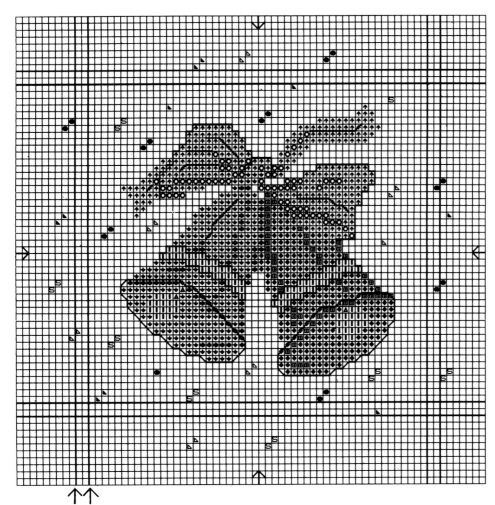

Stitching lines for the gold embroidery thread.

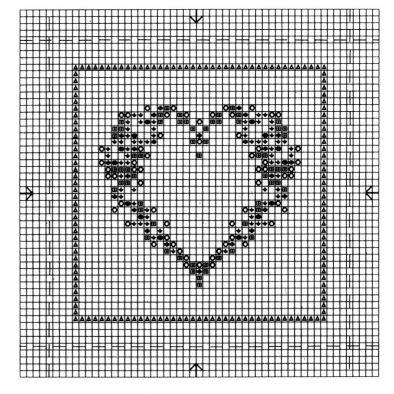

WEDDING
ANNIVERSARY ◀

◆ 762 off-white
△ silver thread, plus
      bks around bells
↑ 3047 pale yellow
○ 676 yellow
◺ 725 rich yellow
| gold thread
      (and double-
      line border)
● 3354 pink
S 747 pale blue
◣ 504 pale green
⊡ 415 grey
      (and bks off-
      white bell)
↓ 928 pale green
      grey
✱ 927 green grey
      (and bks
      green-grey
      bell)

VALENTINE ▶

↓ 962 pink
● 601 red
○ 704 bright green
△ 733 olive green
⊡ 732 dark olive green
✱ 520 dark green

— — — Withdrawn thread line for ribbons.

Lacy Lavender Sachets

Sweet-scented lavender sachets are a traditional idea that will surely never go out of fashion.

These have been designed to be placed in a drawer, but if you wish to make them for use in hanging cupboards (perhaps to accompany a gift of padded coat hangers), you will need to purchase a slightly longer length of ribbon than the amount specified.

Although they are always called lavender sachets, remember that they can be filled with any type of pot pourri. A summer garden mixture with rose petals would be particularly appropriate for the roses and violets design, for example. Alternatively, the strong, lemony scent of southernwood *(Artemisia abrotanum)* is a traditional defence against moths.

LACY LAVENDER
SACHETS

YOU WILL NEED

For one sachet, with an overall measurement of
23cm × 15cm (9in × 6in):

*50cm × 20cm (20in × 8in) of white openweave
fabric, such as cotton Davosa or natural linen,
18 threads to 2.5cm (1in)
32.5cm (13in) of pre-gathered white lace trim,
4cm (1½in) wide
70cm (28in) of double-sided white satin ribbon,
1cm (³⁄₈in) wide
DMC stranded embroidery cotton in the colours
given in the appropriate panel
No26 tapestry needle
Matching sewing thread
Sufficient lavender or pot pourri to fill the
sachet halfway*

•

THE EMBROIDERY

To transfer the positioning lines to the embroidery,
fold the fabric widthways in half and mark this line
with a pin. Measure 8cm (3in) in from this point
and baste across. Baste the upright centre line.

With the fabric held in a hoop, follow the chart
and complete the motif, using two strands of thread
in the needle. Where several colours are required,
and to save time in starting and finishing, you may
prefer to keep two or three needles in use, pinning
them to the side when those particular colours are
not being used.

Remove the basting stitches and steam press the
finished embroidery on the wrong side.

MAKING UP THE SACHET

With the wrong side facing out, fold the fabric
widthways in half; baste and machine stitch the
sides, taking a 2.5cm (1in) seam. If the edges have
frayed, check that the width of the sachet is 15cm
(6in). Trim the seam allowances to 12mm (½in),
and turn to the right side. Make a 4cm (1½in)
single turning on the top edge and baste.

Join the short edges of the lace trim, using a tiny
french seam. Pin and baste the trim to the inside
of the top edge and, working from the right side,
machine stitch in place, sewing close to the top
edge.

Half fill the sachet with lavender or pot pourri
and tie the ribbon twice around the top, finishing
with the bow in front.

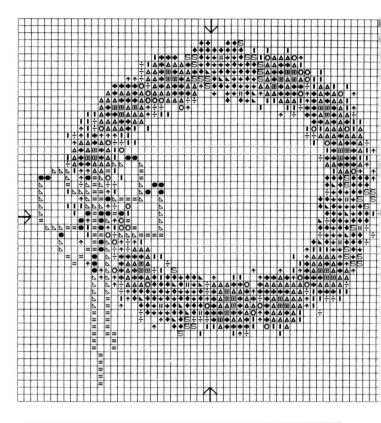

THE ROSE IS RED ▲

‖	445 yellow	✦	792 violet
△	3733 pink	=	3761 turquoise
✱	603 magenta	÷	959 veridian green
⊡	817 dark red	S	943 dark green
◆	341 pale blue	I	989 green
◿	794 blue	↑	471 olive
●	798 deep blue	○	3051 dark olive
◣	3609 mauve		

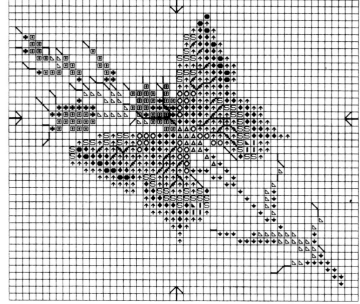

BUTTERFLY, BUTTERFLY ▲

↑ 445 yellow	◺ 989 green
◣ 783 ochre	↓ 993 veridian green
I 721 orange	○ 930 dark green blue
◆ 734 khaki (bks wing)	S 340 light blue
⊡ 602 pink	● 792 dark blue
✳ 349 red	△ 824 navy blue

MARY, MARY ▲

- ‖ white (bks bloomers 930, collar 794)
- ◇ 745 pale lemon (bks butterfly wing 783)
- ✕ 445 pale yellow
- ◺ 444 bright yellow
- ◆ 783 deep yellow
- ↑ 948 flesh (bks cockle shells 783)
- ⊡ 605 pink
- ● 603 deep pink
- ✳ 3705 red
- = 3761 pale blue
- ⬓ 3766 turquoise
- ↓ 930 slate grey (bks butterfly body)
- I 794 blue
- S 564 pale green
- △ 958 veridian green
- ÷ 3348 green
- ◣ 702 dark green
- ○ 3053 khaki

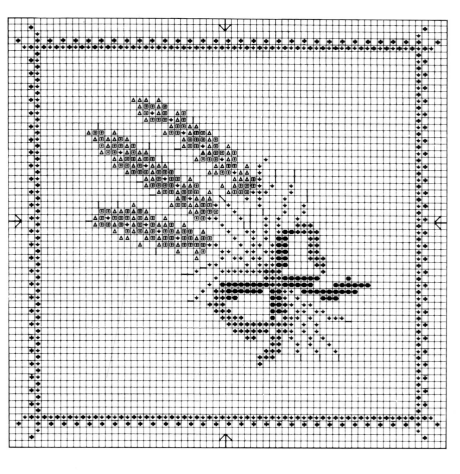

LAVENDER BLUE ▶

✳ 224 pink	△ 341 blue
● 892 geranium	↓ 368 green
⊡ 340 violet	(bks stems)

Tea-Time Tray

When guests call for tea, enchant
them with this delightful tray, with its
beautifully embroidered picture,
safely protected under a glass surface.
The theme – Anthony Rowley, the
cheerful young frog, bearing an
impressive bunch of flowers and about
to call on Miss Mouse – would make
this an amusing gift to bring to an
engagement party. Instead of a tray,
you might use it for the cover of a
wedding-photo album.

A FROG HE WOULD A-WOOING GO ▲

6 white	⊟ 3325 pale blue	△ 830 drab brown
L 727 yellow	I 312 dark blue	↓ 613 stone (and bks 611*)
◇ gold thread	A 734 light olive	T 415 pale grey
÷ 676 gold	(and bks 730*)	= 414 steel grey (bks 310)
◸ 680 deep gold	‖ 523 green	◤ 317 dark grey
⊢ 754 pale pink	◆ 367 dark green	● 310 black (bks 317)
(bks 352)	↑ 520 dark drab green	*Note: 2 additional*
⊡ 758 pink	S 435 light brown	*backstitch colours*
✱ 355 red	○ 832 golden brown	

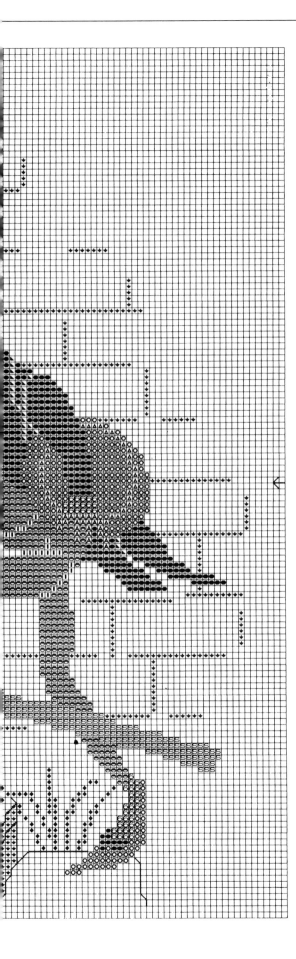

TEA-TIME TRAY

YOU WILL NEED

For a tray measuring 24cm (9½in) square:

30cm (12in) square of cream evenweave
Hardanger, 18 threads to 2.5cm (1in)
DMC stranded embroidery cotton in the colours
given in the panel
No26 tapestry needle
Masking tape or strong thread for securing the
mounted fabric
Square wooden tray (for suppliers, see page 160)

●

THE EMBROIDERY

With the prepared fabric stretched in an embroidery frame (see page 7) begin the cross stitching, using two strands of thread in the needle. Embroider the main characters first and then the background.

Finish by adding the backstitch details, using a single strand of thread.

Remove the design from the frame and steam press on the wrong side, if necessary.

ASSEMBLING THE TRAY

Using a soft pencil, mark the supplied mounting card both ways along the centre. This will help you to position the card exactly in the middle of the embroidery. Place the embroidery face down with the card on top and with the pencil lines and basting stitches matching.

Working on one side and then the opposite side, fold over the edges of the fabric on all sides, and secure with one or two pieces of masking tape. When you are sure the design is centred (if not, simply release the masking tape and adjust the fabric until it is correctly positioned), secure the corners firmly.

Turn in each corner to form a mitre (see page 9), and secure with masking tape. Next, finish securing the sides, stretching the fabric evenly, and finally, overcast the mitred corners to finish. Insert the mounted embroidery into the tray, following the manufacturer's instructions.

Traditional Dressing Table Set

Ideal for any number of occasions –
such as an 18th birthday, an
engagement, or a wedding – this
traditional dressing-table set makes
a very special gift.

We have used a blue background
fabric for the embroidery, but you
might decide to choose an alternative
colour to suit the decor of the
recipient's bedroom. If you opt for
cream, it might be a good idea to
outline the white areas, such as the
ladies' mob caps and the baby's lacy
pillow, in a mid-grey backstitch, to
distinguish them from the
background.

Any of these pictures could be used
to make a card for a special person.
The sleeping baby, for example,
would make a beautiful little card/gift
to send a new mother (traditionalists
can leave the bonnet unstitched until
the baby has arrived, and then pick
the appropriate colour).

TRADITIONAL DRESSING-TABLE SET

YOU WILL NEED

For the dressing-table set – handmirror with back measuring 13cm × 11.5cm (5in × 4½in), hairbrush with back measuring 10cm × 9cm (4in × 3½in), trinket box with lid measuring 10cm (4in) across:

45cm × 20cm (18in × 8in) of blue evenweave fabric (Aida 503), 18 threads to 2.5cm (1in)
DMC stranded embroidery cotton in the colours given in the panels
No26 tapestry needle
Dressing-table set, plus trinket box (for suppliers, see page 160)

•

THE EMBROIDERY

You may find it best to work all three designs on one piece of fabric, stretched in a rectangular frame. In either case, use basting stitches to divide the area into three equal sections measuring 20cm × 15cm (8in × 6in).

Baste the central positioning lines on each section, ready for cross stitching the motifs. Use two strands of thread throughout, with the exception of the star eyelets on the trinket box, which are worked in a single strand. Remove the finished embroidery from the frame and, if necessary, steam press on the wrong side.

ASSEMBLING THE DRESSING-TABLE SET

The paper templates supplied by the manufacturers may vary in size so, in order to get an exact fit for each piece, cut out the embroidery, using the template supplied with each piece, but first mark the centre on the template both ways in pencil. Place the template with the marked side on the wrong side of the embroidery; match the pencil lines to the basting stitches, and draw around with a soft pencil. Before cutting out, place the template inside the frame and check to see how much more fabric, if any, should be included beyond the pencil

line. Cut out the fabric and remove the basting stitches. Complete the assembly of all three pieces, following the manufacturer's instructions.

STAR EYELET

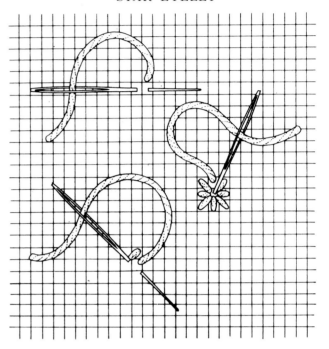

Beginning at the top right corner, work eight straight stitches over two threads (the length of the particular cross stitch being worked), working from the outer edge into the centre, as shown in the diagram.

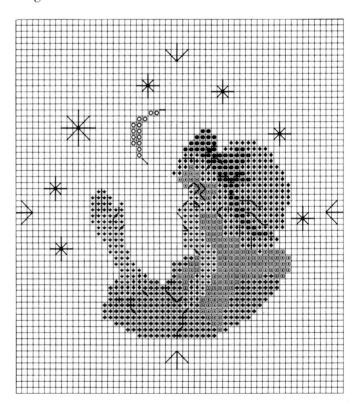

CURLY-LOCKS ◄

◺ white (bks 452)
⊡ 452 stone
S 3078 yellow (bks 734)
◆ 734 ochre (bks 3052)
◣ 754 flesh (bks 224)
✦ 224 pink
✳ 352 deep pink (bks
    embroidery thread)
● 798 blue
○ 3053 green
△ 3052 sage

SLEEP BABY, SLEEP ▼

◺ white	◣ 800 blue
S 834 yellow (and stars)	● 798 dark blue
△ 3045 ochre	I 3347 green
○ 754 flesh (bks	(bks 3052)
eye 3045)	◆ 3072 grey (bks
✳ 3354 pink	legs 798)
⊡ 3328 red (and	*Note: one additional*
bks 3052 *)	*backstitch colour **

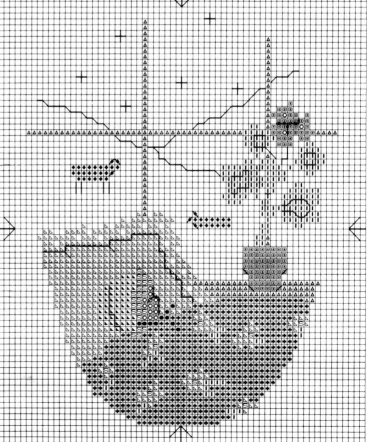

TWINKLE, TWINKLE ◄

◆ white (and bks 793*)
○ 3078 lemon (and eyelet stitch stars)
⊡ 676 yellow
✦ 754 flesh (bks 3354)
✳ 3354 pink (and bks eye)
● 899 red (bks 793)
    Note: one additional backstitch
    colour; stitch the eye as shown below:*
I 793 blue (one upright bks eye)

Christmas Tree Toys

Easily made from oddments of evenweave fabric, these brightly coloured tree toys, with their cross-stitched motifs stretched over cardboard shapes and with gold cord ties, take very little time to make. You can repeat the same motifs, or add your own designs, until you have sufficient toys to fill your Christmas tree. Alternatively, you might prefer to make a small selection each year, and in that way gradually build up your collection.

CHRISTMAS TREE TOYS

YOU WILL NEED

For the Candle and Bell, each measuring 9cm (3½in) across:

Two 13cm (5in) squares of evenweave fabric, 14 threads to 2.5cm (1in), one in pale green (candle) and one in pale blue (bell)
DMC stranded embroidery cotton in the colours given in the appropriate panels
Two circles, 9cm (3½in) in diameter, of 3mm (⅛in) cardboard and two of lightweight synthetic batting, cut to the same size
114cm (1¼yd) of gold cord, 3mm (⅛in) thick
No24 tapestry needle
Matching sewing thread

For the Christmas tree and Santa Claus, each measuring approximately 11cm × 10cm (4½in × 4in):

Two 18cm × 15cm (7¼in × 6in) rectangles of evenweave fabric, 14 threads to 2.5cm (1in), one in pale yellow (Santa Claus) and one in red (Christmas tree)
DMC stranded embroidery cotton in the colours given in the appropriate panels
Two 13cm × 10cm (5in × 4in) rectangles of 3mm (⅛in) cardboard, and two of lightweight synthetic batting, cut to the same size
140cm (1½yd) of gold cord, 3mm (⅛in) thick
No24 tapestry needle
Matching sewing thread

THE EMBROIDERY

All four of these Christmas tree hanging decorations are embroidered and made up in the same way: stretch the prepared fabric in a small hoop, (see page 6) and following the appropriate chart and colour key, complete the embroidery, using two strands of thread in the needle throughout. When you have finished, press the embroidery on the wrong side, retaining the basting stitches that mark the centre lines.

MAKING UP THE TOYS

Following the chart, draw the outline of the appropriate toy on the cardboard, marking the arrows, and cut out. Place the card shape on the batting, aligning the arrows; draw around it with a pencil, and cut it out. Mark the centre both ways on one side of the cardboard – you can place it on the outline given with the chart and pencil-mark the edge.

Lay the embroidery face down; centre the card on top, with basting and pencil lines matching, and lightly draw around. Draw a second line 12mm (½in) outside and trim to this line. Cut the backing fabric to this shape.

Lay the embroidery face down, centring the batting and cardboard on top. Neatly fold over the edges and hold them with adhesive tape. Remove

CHRISTMAS TREE ▼		✲ 602 magenta
◆ 677	pale yellow (bks 606*)	⊡ 3753 pale blue
○ 972	yellow	△ 911 green (and bks tree)
✦ 976	ochre	*Note: one additional bks colour*

the basting threads, then turn in the edges of the backing fabric and pin them to the back. Using matching sewing thread, slipstitch around the edge.

Cut the cord into two equal lengths. Fold one length in half to find the central point and pin this to the centre of the bottom edge of the toy. Pin the cord around the toy, leaving the two long ends at the centre top for tying to the tree. Slipstitch around, firmly oversewing the join at the centre top of the toy.

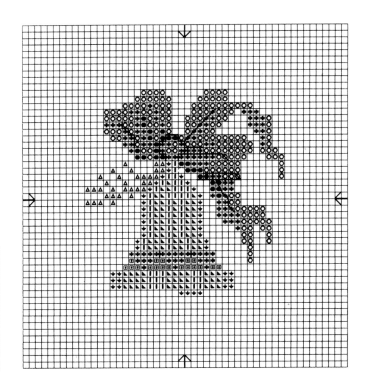

BELL ▶

◣	3078 lemon yellow	✱	224	dusky pink
I	743 yellow	●	961	deep pink
↓	972 deep yellow	⊡	799	blue
○	605 pink (bks 961)	△	911	green

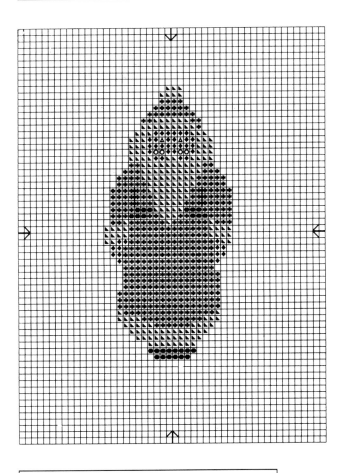

CANDLE ▼

⊃	712 cream (and bks 928)	●	606	red
◣	743 pale yellow (bks 972)	✱	602	magenta
		△	958	veridian green (bks veins 911)
○	972 yellow	↓	911	green
◆	605 pink	⊡	928	grey

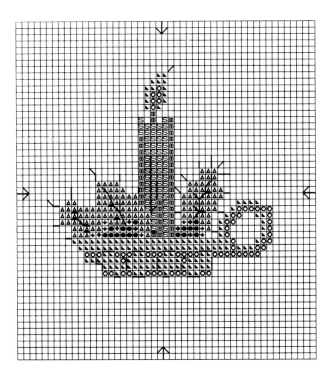

SANTA CLAUS ▲

◣	white	✱	606 red (bks 3799)
◆	948 flesh		
○	961 pink	△	799 blue
		●	3799 black

Christmas Greetings Cards

What better way to personalize your Christmas greetings than to embroider them yourself? Using prepared mounts, you can give them a truly professional finish. Once Christmas is over, the card mounts can be framed, so perhaps you might give a suitable frame as an accompanying gift. Three traditional Christmas rhymes – 'Little Jack Horner', 'Dame get up and bake your pies', and 'I saw three ships come sailing by' – have been used, but only the dame, with her Christmas decorations up, presents a very clearly Christmassy image. Either the three ships, or even Jack Horner, could be used for a birthday card, and the former would make a lovely parting gift for friends or family going to live abroad.

CHRISTMAS GREETINGS CARDS

YOU WILL NEED

For the *Little Jack Horner* card, measuring overall 20cm × 14.5cm (8in × 5¾in), with rectangular portrait cut out, 14cm × 9.5cm (5½in × 3¾in):

*23cm × 18cm (9in × 7¼in) of blue evenweave
fabric (Aida), 18 threads to 2.5cm (1in)
DMC stranded embroidery cotton in the colours
given in the appropriate panel
No26 tapestry needle
Card mount (for suppliers, see page 160)*

For the *Dame Get Up* card, measuring overall 20cm × 14cm (8in × 5½in) with oval portrait cut out, 14cm × 9.5cm (5½in × 3¾in):

*23cm × 18cm (9in × 7¼in) of white evenweave
cotton (Linda), 27 threads to 2.5cm (1in)
DMC stranded embroidery cotton in the colours
given in the appropriate panel
No26 tapestry needle
Card mount (for suppliers, see page 160)*

For the *I Saw Three Ships* card, measuring overall 20cm × 14.5cm (8in × 5¾in) with rectangular landscape cut out, 14cm × 9.5cm (5½in × 3¾in):

*23cm × 18cm (9in × 7¼in) of white (natural)
linen, 26 threads to 2.5cm (1in)
DMC stranded embroidery cotton in the colours
given in the appropriate panel
No26 tapestry needle
Card mount (for suppliers, see page 160)*

•

THE EMBROIDERY

Prepare the fabric for each individual card in the same way and stretch it in a hoop (see page 6).

Bear in mind that very openweave linens tend to fray, so it is a good idea to overcast the edges beforehand.

Complete the cross stitching, using two strands of thread in the needle throughout. Finish by adding the backstitch details, using a single strand of thread. Remove the embroidery from the frame; take out the basting stitches, and steam press on the wrong side.

ASSEMBLING THE CARDS

Open out the self-adhesive card mount; centre your embroidered design over the window; trim to size, and fold over the left-hand side section. Press to secure.

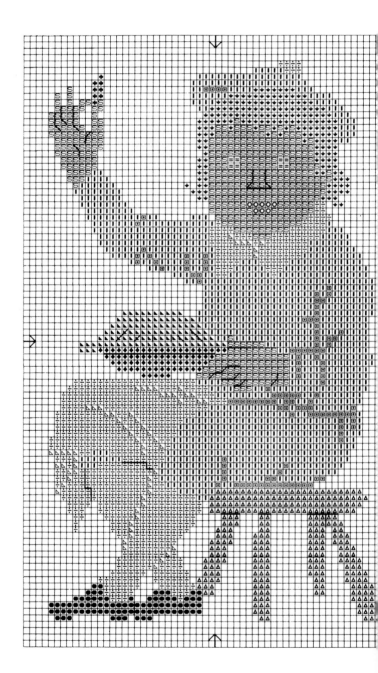

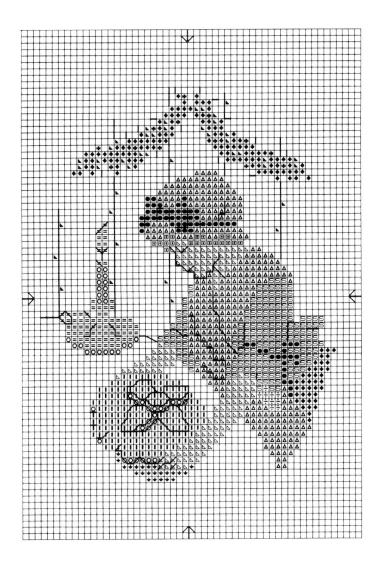

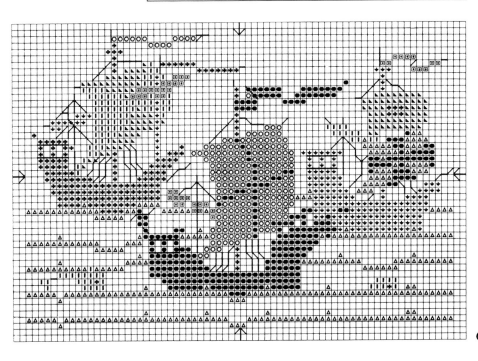

Traditional Sampler

The enduring appeal of the sampler –
worked here in the traditional style,
with borders and motifs in a single
colour – will ensure that this
delightful picture of the twelve
princesses becomes a favourite gift
for family and friends.
The sampler is designed to be
mounted in a frame, but if you choose
to embroider this design as a tray
cloth or table runner you
could easily increase the size
by setting the pairs of princesses
further away from the central
image of the magical night-time
castle, with its mysterious lake.

DANCING PRINCESSES ▲

3047 cream (bks on castle walls)   ● 349 red (and bks details)

TRADITIONAL SAMPLER

YOU WILL NEED

For a sampler measuring 24cm × 29cm
(9½in × 11½in):

*35cm × 40cm (14in × 16in) of pale khaki
evenweave Aida fabric, or linen,
16 threads to 2.5cm (1in)
DMC stranded emboidery cotton in the colour given
in the panel, plus 3 skeins of red 349, used for
the main colour
No24 tapestry needle
24cm × 29cm (9½in × 11½in) of lightweight
synthetic batting
24cm × 29cm (9½in × 11½in) of
medium-weight mounting board
Spray glue
Picture frame of your choice*

•

THE EMBROIDERY

With the prepared fabric stretched in a frame (see page 7) and the centre lines basted both ways, begin the embroidery. Using two strands of thread in the needle, and carefully following the chart, complete the cross stitching.

Remove the finished embroidery from the frame; take out the basting stitches, and steam press the work on the wrong side.

FRAMING THE SAMPLER

For a slightly padded effect, a thin layer of batting is placed between the embroidery and the mounting board. Cut the batting to the same size as the mounting board and attach it to the board with spray glue or fabric adhesive. Mount the embroidery, following the instructions given for heavier fabrics on page 9.

Insert the glass and the mounted embroidery into your picture frame; add the backing board provided, and tack in place. Cover the tacks with broad sticky tape to neaten, and your sampler is ready to hang up.

Wedding Day Treasures

This exquisite ringbearer's cushion, embroidered with doves, flowers, hearts and the bride's and groom's initials, and surrounded with delicate floral borders and lace trim, is teamed with two charming well-wisher's confetti/rice bags. Edged and tied with ribbon bows, these little bags would make pretty purses after the wedding – looped on a sash in pocket-purse style – and all three pieces would become treasured mementoes of the day.

WEDDING-DAY TREASURES

For a Ringbearer's cushion measuring 25cm (10in) square (including lace trim):

Two 20cm (8in) squares of white evenweave linen or Davosa, 26 threads to 2.5cm (1in)
DMC stranded embroidery cotton in the colours given in the appropriate panel
76cm (30in) of white pre-gathered lace trim, 4cm (1½in) wide
20cm (8in) square cushion pad
Two 46cm (18in) lengths of parcel ribbon, one in blue and one in pale pink
No26 tapestry needle
Matching sewing threads

For the Well-wisher's confetti/rice bags, each measuring approximately 13cm × 10cm (5in × 4in):

Two 33cm × 12cm (13in × 4½in) pieces of white evenweave linen or Davosa, 26 threads to 2.5cm (1in)
DMC stranded embroidery cotton in the colours given in the appropriate panels
Two 90cm (1yd) lengths of satin ribbon, 12mm (½in) wide, one in pale blue and one in pale pink
No26 tapestry needle
Matching sewing thread
Tracing paper

•

THE RING-BEARER'S CUSHION

With the prepared fabric stretched in a hoop (see page 6) begin the embroidery, using two strands of thread in the needle and working one cross stitch over two threads of ground fabric throughout. Following the chart and colour key, begin with the inner border and finish with the outer border. Using 955, make an eye with a french knot, two stitches back from the beak, on each bird. Complete the embroidery and remove it from the hoop. Take out the basting stitches and steam press on the wrong side, if needed.

MAKING UP THE CUSHION

Using a tiny french seam, join the raw short edges of the lace trim together. Lay the lace on the embroidery, facing inward and with right sides together, and baste the edge of the lace to the outer edge of the fabric, just inside the 12mm (½in) seam allowance. Ease the gathers around the edges, allowing a little extra fullness at the corners. Machine stitch in place.

With right sides together, place the backing fabric on top. Baste and machine stitch around, leaving a 13cm (5in) opening in the middle of one side. Trim across the corners and turn the cover through to the right side.

Fold the lengths of parcel ribbon in half and stitch the folds to the centre of the cushion, in readiness for tying on the wedding rings.

Insert the cushion pad, turn in the edges of the opening and slipstitch to close.

THE HEART-SHAPED CONFETTI BAG

Fold the prepared fabric widthways in half and cut along the fold. Set one section (the back) aside, and on the other mark the centre both ways with basting stitches. Stretch the fabric in a hoop and, referring to the chart, complete the embroidery, using two strands of thread in the needle and working one cross stitch over two threads throughout. Steam press the finished embroidery on the wrong side.

MAKING UP THE BAG

Using a soft pencil, trace the outline of the heart and mark the centre lines, as on the chart. Lay the embroidery face down. Turn over the tracing and place it on the embroidery, with basting and pencil lines matching, then go over the outline to transfer it to the fabric. Working freehand, draw a second line 12mm (½in) outside, for the seam allowance, and cut out the fabric. Using this as a template, cut out the backing fabric.

Cut a 25cm (10in) length of ribbon for the handle, and put this to one side. Join the raw ends of the remaining ribbon together, using a tiny french seam. Pleat the ribbon and pin it to the right side of the embroidery, in the same way as the lace trim for the Ring-bearer's cushion. With the embroidery and backing fabric right sides together, machine stitch around the edge, leaving the opening, as marked on the chart.

Turn and hem a 6mm (¼in) double turning on the top edge of the backing.

For the handle, fold the remaining ribbon and attach the two ends inside the top front edge with a few back stitches, taken through the seam allowance. Make a buttonhole loop inside the hem opposite. Fill the bag with confetti, then thread the handle through the loop.

THE STRAIGHT-SIDED CONFETTI BAG

Following the diagram on page 75, fold the fabric widthways in half and mark the foldline with basting stitches. In the top section only, baste the vertical centre to give the positioning lines for the embroidery. Referring to the chart, complete the embroidery as for the heart-shaped bag.

MAKING UP THE BAG

With right sides together, fold the fabric widthways in half and baste the two sides. Machine stitch,

using matching sewing thread. Trim the seams to 6mm (¼in) and press open. Make a 12mm (½in) double turning on the top edge; pin; baste, and hem to secure.

For the handle, cut 40cm (16in) of pink ribbon and tuck the ends inside the bag, catchstitching them to the centre front and back, about 3cm (1¼in) in from the edge (where the stitches will be hidden under the tied bow). Fold the remaining ribbon in half and attach it to the side of the bag, about 3cm (1¼in) down from the top edge. Fill the bag with confetti or rice and tie the ribbon in a bow to finish.

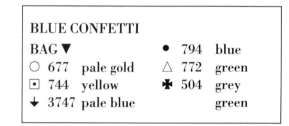

BLUE CONFETTI			
BAG ▼		• 794	blue
○ 677	pale gold	△ 772	green
⊡ 744	yellow	✳ 504	grey
✦ 3747	pale blue		green

Leave open

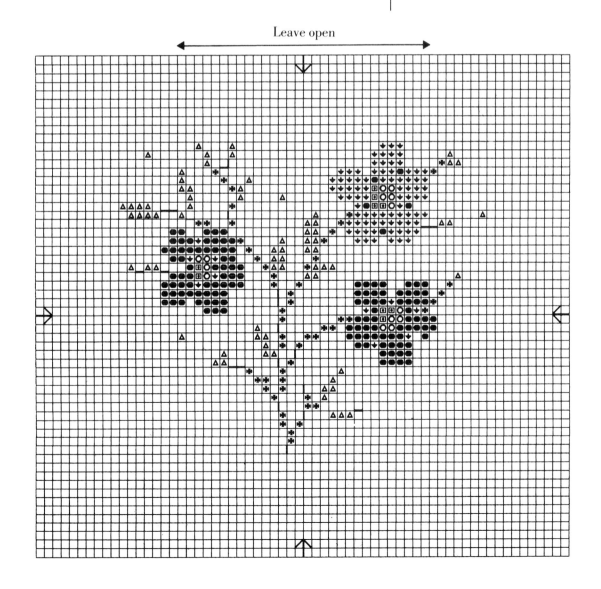

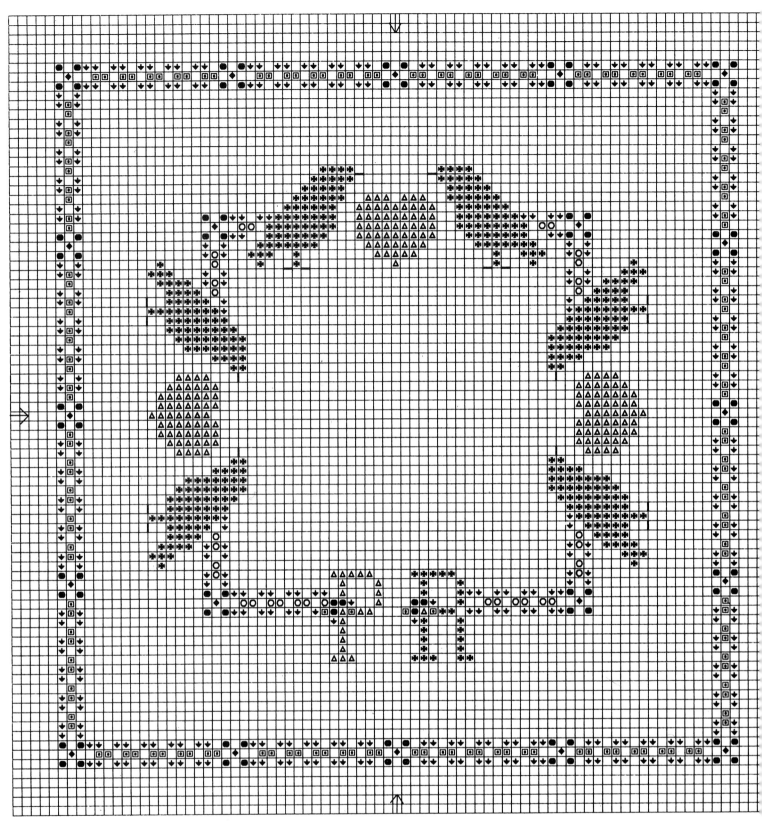

WEDDING RING

PILLOW▲

◆　677　yellow

△　605　pink

●　963　deep pink

✳　3747　blue

⊡　955　mint green

↓　722　yellow green

○　504　grey green

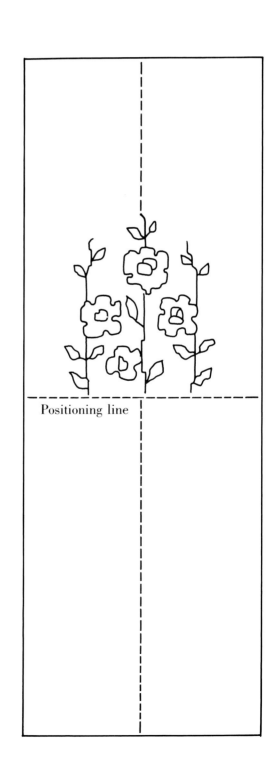

Positioning line

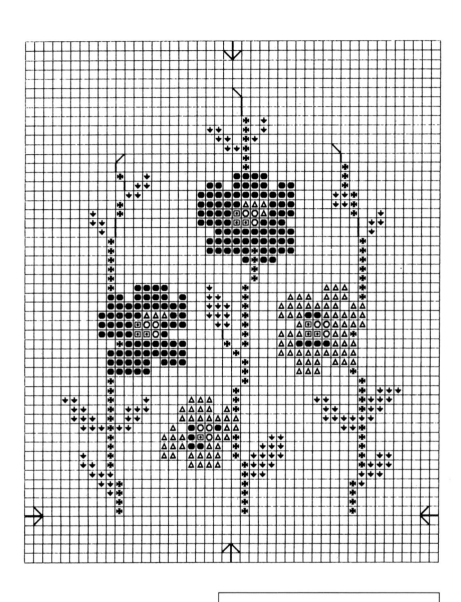

PINK CONFETTI BAG ▲

○   677   pale gold
⊡   744   yellow
△   605   pale pink
●   962   pink
↓   722   green
✠   504   grey green

Victorian Mounts

Capturing the Victorian style of decorated picture mounts, these can be used to give a traditional effect to whatever you may wish to frame. The right-hand frame incorporates pearl beads in the shoe buckles and the elves' eyes, and the roses of the left-hand frame are similarly decorated. If you wish to set these behind glass, you could substitute stitches in a darker shade on the first, and omit beads from the roses.

VICTORIAN MOUNTS

YOU WILL NEED

For one picture mount with an overall measurement of 24cm × 19cm (9½in × 7½in); this includes 6mm (¼in) all around, for fitting into the recess of a picture frame:

*30cm × 25cm (12in × 10in) of cream linen,
26 threads to 2.5cm (1in)
DMC stranded embroidery cotton in the colours
given in the appropriate panel
24cm × 19cm (9½in × 7½in) of lightweight
synthetic batting
30cm × 25cm (12in × 10in) of lightweight
iron-on interfacing
24cm × 19cm (9½ × 7½in) of thin
mounting card
Craft knife or sharp general purpose scissors
No26 tapestry needle and No9 crewel needle
Matching sewing threads
Tracing paper
Spray glue
All-purpose clear glue
Picture frame of your choice with a window area
measuring 23cm × 18cm (9in × 7in)*

•

THE EMBROIDERY

All three mounts are made in the same way. Stretch the fabric in a rectangular frame (see page 7). Using two strands of embroidery thread in the needle, and referring to the appropriate chart, complete the cross stitching. Remove the work from the frame and press the interfacing to the wrong side of the fabric. Using the crewel needle and matching thread, add the beads and pearls to the Elves and the Shoemaker and to Snow White and Rose Red respectively. If necessary, gently steam press the finished embroidery on the right side.

COMPLETING THE MOUNT

Using a soft pencil (2B), begin by tracing both the inner and outer lines of the frame given with the chart. Turn over the tracing; centre it on the card, and trace through. Carefully cut out the window area, using a craft knife.

Cut the batting to the same shape as the mount, using the latter as a template, and then attach it to the mount with spray glue.

Mount the fabric, following the instructions for heavier fabrics (see page 9). With the wrong side facing, cut horizontally and vertically, and then cut diagonally across the centre both ways, cutting through both layers and snipping right up to the corners and to within 6mm (¼in) of the window edge. You will find that one or two tiny spots of clear glue, placed at the corners of the card, will help to secure the cut threads of the fabric. Trim across the flaps to straighten them, leaving allowances 12mm (½in) deep. Working on opposite sides, fold the allowances to the back of the card and secure them firmly with masking tape.

Centre your chosen photograph or painting behind the mount, securing it with masking tape before inserting the mount into the picture frame.

STITCHING ON BEADS

Use the same method to attach small, even-shaped beads and pearls.

● Using either a fine crewel needle, number 9 or 10, or a beading straw for very fine beads, and sewing thread or fine silk, bring out the needle and thread on a bead. Reinsert the needle through the same hole, then make a stitch the width of the bead (and in this case, the width of the cross stitch), and pull through, with the thread below the needle. Repeat, completing the design as instructed.

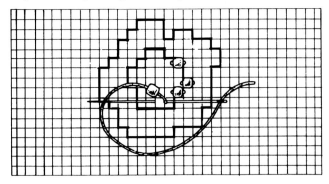

THE GOLDEN BIRD ▶

△ gold thread (bks 3052)
⊡ 3013 green (bks around tree and twigs)
✱ 3053 drab green
● 3052 dark drab green

THE ELVES AND THE SHOEMAKER ▲

⊡   963 pale pink (bks 3733)

△   963 with matching glass beads

●   3733 pink (bks sewing thread; bks 452)

✱   452 drab mauve (bks sewing needles and
      cotton reels)

SNOW WHITE AND ROSE RED ▶

↑   white (bks 452)

╱   white seed pearls

S   726 yellow

I   725 deep yellow

◣   761 pink (bks thorns and stems)

●   352 deep pink (bks around pink flowers)

△   3013 sage green

○   733 green

✱   924 dark green

◆   3072 pale grey

↓   452 grey (bks thorns and stems)

⊡   451 dark grey

Happy Birthday

Naturalistic flowers and fruits, embroidered on backgrounds of a contrast colour, are featured on this charming trio of birthday greetings cards.
Friends and relatives will be delighted to receive them, and cards as pretty as this should be framed after the day and hung as miniature pictures.

HAPPY BIRTHDAY

YOU WILL NEED

For the three Birthday greetings cards, each measuring overall 20cm × 14cm (8in × 5½in), with oval portrait cut outs, 14cm × 9.5cm (5½in × 3¾in):

For the *Rose* card:

23cm × 18cm (9in × 7¼in) of evenweave Linda fabric, 26 threads to 2.5cm (1in), in pale blue
No26 tapestry needle

For the *Flower Basket* card:

23cm × 18cm (9in × 7¼in) of evenweave Linda fabric, 26 threads to 2.5cm (1in), in yellow
No26 tapestry needle

For the *Strawberries* card:

23cm × 18cm (9in × 7¼in) of offwhite linen, 20 threads to 2.5cm (1in)
No18 tapestry needle

For each card:

DMC stranded embroidery cotton in the colours given in the appropriate panel
Card mount (for suppliers, see page 160)

•

THE EMBROIDERY

Prepare the fabric (overcasting the edges and basting the centre both ways) and then stretch it in a hoop (see page 6). For all three designs, work one cross stitch over two threads of fabric. For the Flower Basket and Rose designs, embroider with two strands of thread in the No26 needle throughout. For the Strawberries design, use the No18 needle and three strands of thread throughout. Embroider the stems first, and then the strawberries and leaves.

Steam press the finished embroideries on the wrong side. Leave the basting stitches in place at this stage; they will be used later for centring the design in the card.

ASSEMBLING THE CARDS

Open out the self-adhesive card mount; centre your embroidery over the cut-out window (using the basting threads as accurate guide lines), and trim the fabric until it is some 12mm (½in) larger all around than the marked area on the card. Remove the basting stitches. Reposition your embroidery; fold over the left-hand section of the card, and press to secure.

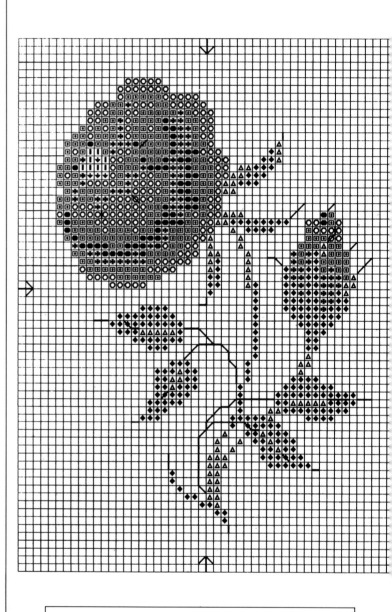

ROSE ▲		
		✿ 602 magenta
I	734 pale yellow	◆ 966 green
↓	972 yellow	(bks 959)
○	605 pale pink	△ 959 veridian
⊡	962 pink	green (and
●	335 warm pink	bks stems)

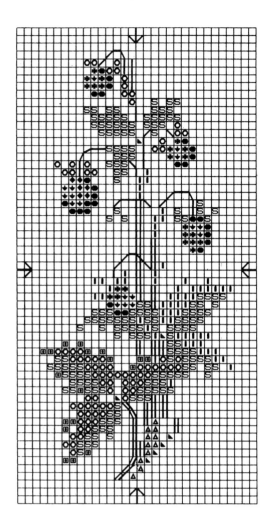

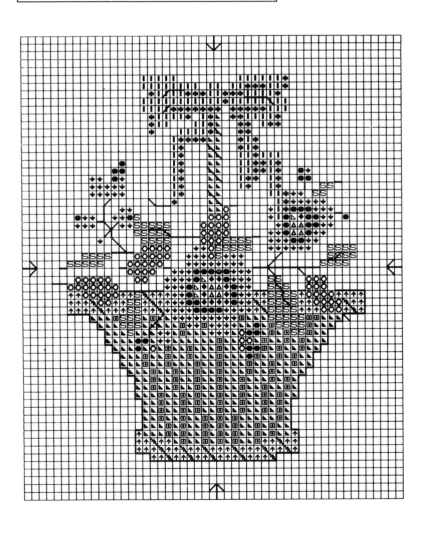

QUICK
and
EASY GIFTS

If you wish you could give your friends and family a gift with a personal touch but simply don't have the time to make anything too elaborate, this chapter is for you. Here you will find a delightful collection of quick and easy gift ideas, including preserve-pot covers, bookmarks and paperweights.

Floral Basket Liner

Embroidered with a simple border of pastel-coloured flowers, this liner, with its pretty scalloped edge, is the perfect accessory for a basket of beautifully-wrapped sweets or petit fours. The edge is bound with a contrasting binding, but you could buttonhole stitch around the edge as an alternative. Embroider the cross stitching first, then the buttonholing; finally, trim the fabric up to the outer twisted edge of the stitching.

FLORAL
BASKET LINER

YOU WILL NEED

For a Basket liner, measuring 30cm × 25cm
(12in × 10in):

*34cm × 29cm (13½in × 11½in) of white linen,
28 threads to 2.5cm (1in)
DMC stranded embroidery cotton in the colours
given in the panel
No26 tapestry needle
115cm (1¼yd) of contrast cotton bias binding,
12mm (½in) wide
Sewing thread to match the contrast binding
15cm (6in) square of cardboard for a template
(use a breakfast cereal box, or similar packaging)
Tracing paper*

THE EMBROIDERY

Stretch the prepared fabric in a frame and, following the chart, cross stitch the motifs given in one
quarter section, as marked by the basting stitches.
Use two strands of thread in the needle and work
one cross stitch over two threads of fabric throughout. For the remaining three sections, turn the frame
through 90 degrees and repeat the cross stitching.

Remember not to strand the thread across the
back of the fabric, or it will show through on the
right side. Remove the finished embroidery from
the frame, retaining the basting stitches, and steam
press on the wrong side.

DRAWING THE SCALLOPED EDGE

Using a soft pencil, trace the outline of the quarter
section, as shown, and transfer it to the cardboard
(to do this, simply turn the tracing over and,
placing it on the cardboard, pencil over the back
of the outline). Cut out the template.

Lay the embroidery face down and position the
template over one quarter section, matching the
straight lines to the basted lines. Lightly draw

around the scalloped edge with a pencil. Repeat for
the other three quarter sections, cut around the
scalloped edge, and remove the basting stitches.

BINDING THE EDGE

With right sides and raw edges together, pin and
baste the binding around the edge (see page 8),

To complete the embroidery, turn the fabric through 90 degrees and repeat the design three times.

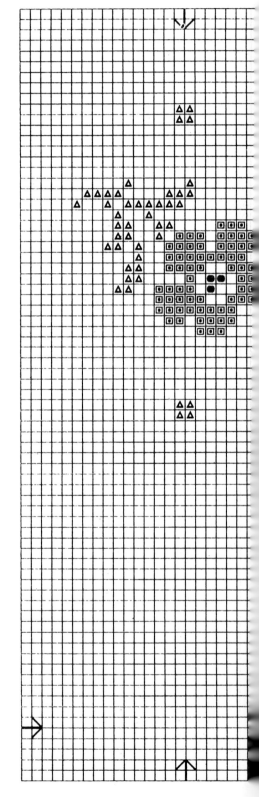

beginning in the corner of one scallop. Where the two ends of the binding meet, overlap by 2cm (¾in), turning the raw, overlapped end under by 6mm (¼in) to neaten it. Using matching sewing thread, machine stitch or backstitch in place.

Turn the binding over the edge of the fabric, and hem, sewing into the back of the first stitching to prevent the thread from showing through.

FLORAL BASKET LINER ▼

✚	725	yellow
✱	961	pink
●	326	dark red
⊡	341	blue
△	733	olive green

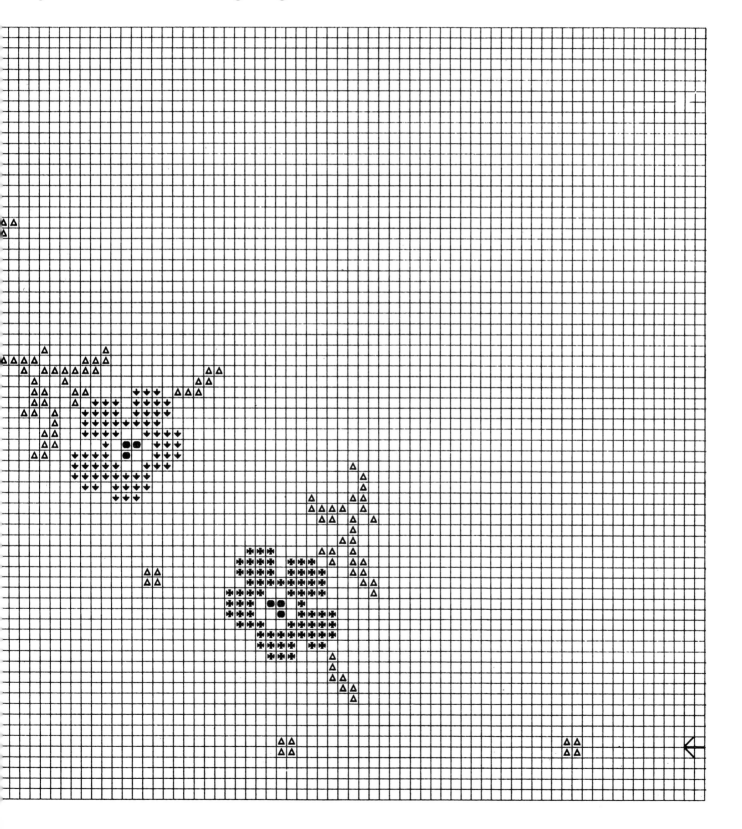

Paper-weights

Made from small remnants of linen, these charming little paperweights are perfect starting points for beginners. Featuring those two well-known opposites, the sophisticated town mouse and the simple country mouse, they would make ideal designs for a child to stitch, perhaps as a gift for a grandmother or a favourite aunt. Alternatively, the two designs, set in either brass or silvered frames, would make a pretty pair of pictures for a small child's room.

PAPERWEIGHTS

YOU WILL NEED

For two paperweights, one an oval measuring
10cm × 8cm (4in × 3in), and the other circular,
measuring 9cm (3½in) in diameter:

*25cm × 15cm (10in × 6in) of natural linen,
21 threads to 2.5cm (1in)
DMC stranded embroidery cotton in the colours
given in the appropriate panel
No26 tapestry needle
Glass-topped paperweights
(for suppliers, see page 160)*

THE EMBROIDERY

If you are embroidering both designs on one piece
of fabric, begin by preparing the edges and stretching it in a rectangular frame. Otherwise, divide the
fabric in half, overcast the edges, and set each
piece in a hoop.

Baste the centre both ways for each design.
Following the charts and colour keys, complete
the embroidery, using two strands of thread in
the needle throughout. Work the cross stitching
first and then finish with the backstitch details.
Remember when embroidering on very openweave
fabric not to strand across the back, otherwise the
threads will be visible on the right side. Remove
the finished embroidery from the frame and steam
press on the wrong side.

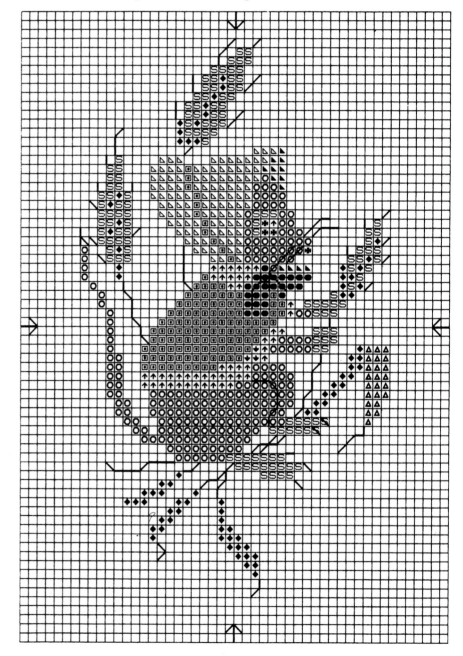

COUNTRY MOUSE ▶

↑ white
S 3046 straw (bks feet)
◣ 224 pink
● 3731 deep pink
◺ 828 pale turquoise
⊡ 518 deep turquoise
△ 3053 sap green (bks leaves)
○ 3045 brown (bks 413)
◆ 772 stone (bks corn stems and
   whiskers)
↓ 762 grey
✱ 413 dark grey (bks whiskers)

MOUNTING FABRIC OVER A PAPER TEMPLATE

The manufacturer suggests mounting the cut-out embroidery and securing it underneath with the felt backing supplied. This is a suitable method for fine fabrics, but with a medium-weight linen, the raw edges can clearly be seen, giving a slightly frayed look. To overcome this, simply mount the fabric over the paper template supplied.

Place the paper template over the chart and mark the centre both ways, using a soft pencil. Lay the embroidery face down with the template on top, matching basting stitches and centre lines. Draw around the edge with the pencil. Working freehand, draw a second line about 2.5cm (1in) outside, and cut out along this line.

Using sewing thread in the needle, make a line of running stitches about 12mm (½in) in from the raw edge. Place the paper template on the wrong side and pull up the thread, spacing the gathers evenly, and making sure the grain of the fabric is straight and the design is centred.

ASSEMBLING THE PAPERWEIGHTS

Following the instructions given for the Drinks Tray on page 111, mount the embroidery, and then finish the assembly, according to manufacturer's instructions.

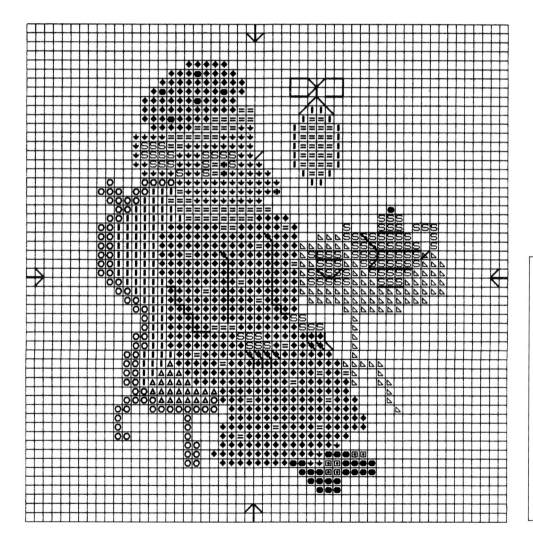

◀ TOWN MOUSE

= white
◣ 3046 straw (bks mirror bow)
S 224 pink (bks fingers)
● 3731 deep pink (bks on teaset)
◆ 598 turquoise (bks 413)
⊡ 518 deep turquoise
△ 3053 sap green
○ 3045 brown
I 772 stone
♦ 762 grey
✳ 413 dark grey (bks eye)

Pretty Pin-
cushions

Pincushions are an essential tool for needleworkers and these three are quick to make and roomy enough to hold a good supply of pins.

One embroidery is set into a purchased cushion on a wooden base, making an attractive gift that might well be left out on display when not in use.

The other two are made like miniature cushions and trimmed, one with simple ribbon bows and the other with fine cord. They would make ideal gifts to bring as a contribution to a fund-raising effort, such as a Christmas crafts fair.

The cord binding was purchased but could have been made from embroidery cotton. To do this, simply cut several long strands; tie them together at one end and secure this to a door handle; twist the other end until the strands are twisted along their entire length, and then hold the centre and bring the two ends together to complete the cord.

PRETTY PINCUSHIONS

YOU WILL NEED

For the *Two Birds* pincushion, measuring 11.5cm (4½in) across:

*18cm (7¼in) square of cream evenweave
Hardanger, 16 threads to 2.5cm (1in)
DMC stranded embroidery cotton in the colours
given in the appropriate panel
No24 tapestry needle
Pincushion mould with wooden surround
(for suppliers, see page 160)*

For the *Little Maiden* pincushion, measuring 13cm (5in) square:

*Two 15cm (6in) squares of cream evenweave
(Aida) fabric, 14 threads to 2.5cm (1in)
110cm (1⅓yds) of pale pink parcel ribbon
DMC stranded embroidery cotton in the colours
given in the appropriate panel
No24 tapestry needle
Sufficient kapok or sheep's wool for filling
Matching sewing thread*

For *Wee Willie Winkie* pincushion, measuring 13cm (5in) square:

*Two 15cm (6in) squares of grey evenweave
(Aida 705) fabric, 18 threads to 2.5cm (1in)
60cm (24in) of narrow, deep turquoise cord
DMC stranded embroidery cotton in the colours
given in the appropriate panel
No26 tapestry needle
Sufficient kapok or sheep's wool for filling
Matching sewing threads*

•

THE EMBROIDERY

Work all three pincushions in the following way. Prepare the fabric and stretch it in a hoop (see page 6) and taking one of the two squares only for the Little Maiden and Wee Willie Winkie. Complete the embroidery, using two strands of thread in the needle. Remove from the frame and steam press on the wrong side.

MAKING UP THE PINCUSHIONS

For the Two Birds cushion, lay the fabric face down, with the wooden base centred on top, and draw around with a soft pencil. Add at least a further 12mm (½in) outside the line and cut out. Run a gathering thread along the pencil line; centre the embroidery over the mould, and pin to hold. Pull up the gathering thread; even out the gathers around the underside of the mould, and secure the thread firmly. Attach the mould to the base with the screw provided.

For the Little Maiden and Wee Willie Winkie cushions, in each case place the two sections right sides together, and then pin and machine stitch around the edge, taking 12mm (½in) seams and leaving an 8cm (3in) opening in one side. Turn right side out and insert the filling. Slipstitch the opening to close.

For the Little Maiden, cut the ribbon into four equal lengths and tie a bow around each corner, taking the ribbon twice around before tying. For Wee Willie Winkie, slipstitch the cord around the edge, looping the cord into a circle approximately 12mm (½in) in diameter at each corner, as shown in the photograph.

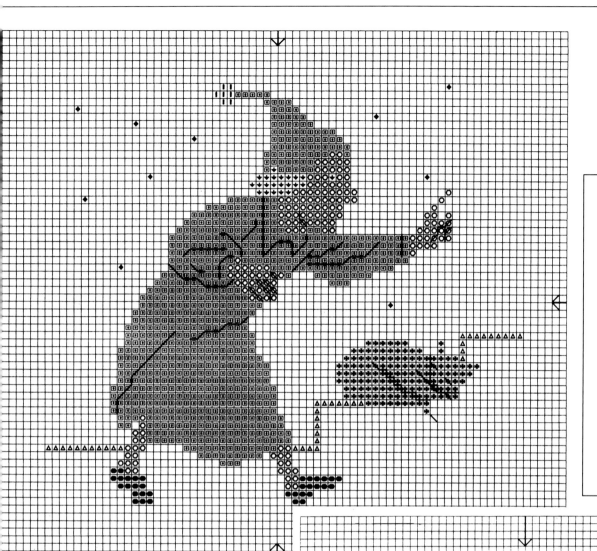

Preserve Pot Covers

Made from washable cotton, these pretty, lace-edged covers are quick and easy to embroider, and will enhance either home-made or store purchased preserves, such as chutneys, mustards, ketchups or pickles.

If you do not have a small embroidery hoop, set a piece of spare fabric in your hoop and secure the pot cover to the centre, stitching around the edge of the inner circle. Taking care not to cut the cover, remove the backing fabric from behind the circle.

PRESERVE-POT COVERS

YOU WILL NEED

For three preserve-pot covers, each measuring 18cm (7¼in) across, with a 6.5cm (2½in) central circle of evenweave Hardanger:

Three lace-edged pot covers with cream evenweave centres, 18 threads to 2.5cm (1in)
(for suppliers, see page 160)
210cm (2⅓yd) of bright pink satin ribbon, 6mm (¼in) wide
DMC stranded emboidery cotton in the colours given in the panels
No26 tapestry needle
Ribbon threader

THE EMBROIDERY

These would make lovely beginner's projects for a child wanting to learn cross stitch. So that they are easy to follow, the charts are shown to a large scale.

All three covers are worked in the same way. With the Hardanger placed centrally in a 10cm (4in) diameter hoop (see page 6), and the centre lines based both ways, you can now begin the embroidery. Following the appropriate chart, complete the cross stitching, using two strands of thread in the needle throughout. Use a single strand to work the backstitching on the mouse's body, the twigs carried by the bird and the hair and tail of the sausage.

Remove the basting stitches and steam press the finished covers on the wrong side.

Cut the ribbon into three equal lengths and, using the ribbon threader, thread it through the holes provided in the lace edging.

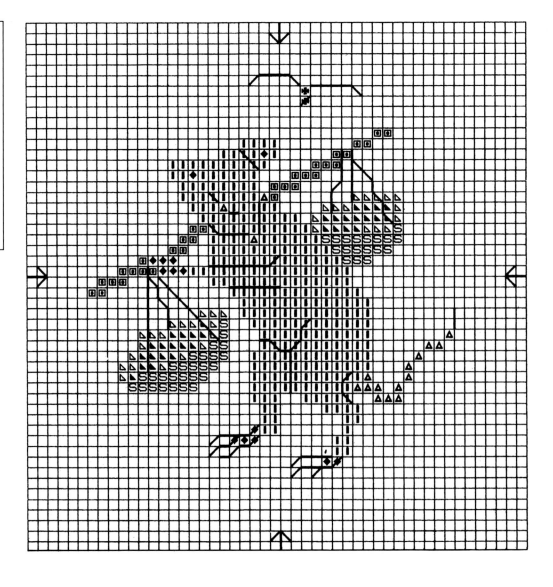

THE MOUSE ►

- ◹ 834 yellow
- ∽ 680 ochre
- ◆ 224 pink
- ▣ 3772 brick red
- ◣ 800 pale blue
- Ⅰ 415 grey (bks 317, including feet)
- △ 317 dark grey (bks on bird and water carriers)

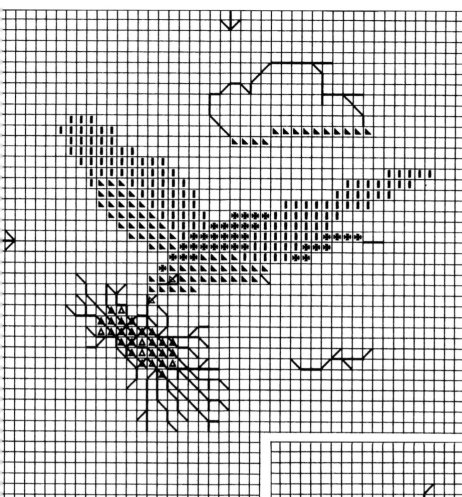

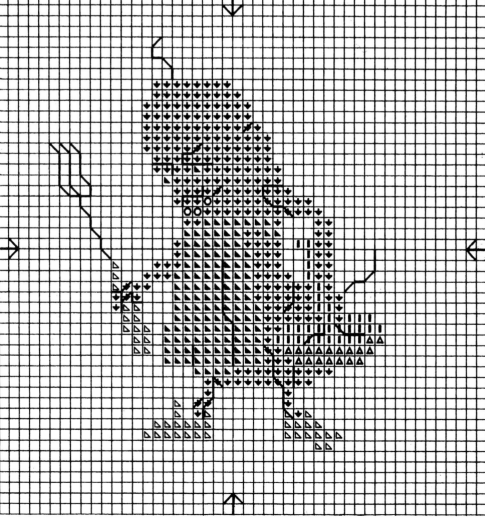

Bordered Guest Towels

Plain linen guest towels are decorated with simple floral motifs, repeated in sequence across one short edge only. Instead of embroidering across the full width, you may prefer to stitch a single motif in each corner of the towel.

To embroider other towelling, first cross stitch the design on a band of evenweave fabric and then hem it in place over the towelling pile.

BORDERED GUEST TOWELS

YOU WILL NEED

For two Guest towels, each measuring
62cm × 37cm (24½in × 14½in):

*Two prepared guest towels, 26 threads to
2.5cm (1in), which can be purchased from
specialist suppliers (see page 160); alternatively,
for applying a band to thick-pile towelling, you
will need evenweave fabric, such as Linda, with
26 threads to 2.5cm (1in), the width of the towel
by 8cm (3in) deep, plus turnings on all sides
DMC stranded embroidery cotton in the colours
given in the panels
No26 tapestry needle
Matching sewing thread for applied band
Narrow lace edging (optional)*

•

THE EMBROIDERY

Embroidering a prepared guest towel is a relatively
easy operation, especially with these repeated
motifs – the most important consideration is to
make sure that you balance the repeats correctly,
starting from the centre.

At the end of the towel to be embroidered, begin
by basting the centre vertically (either count the
threads or measure precisely, and mark with a pin).
The line should ideally be about 15cm (6in) long.
Next, baste the base line across the towel, placing
this line 6cm (2½in) up from the hemstitching of
the fringed edge.

On both designs, work one cross stitch over two
threads of ground fabric. Following the chart and
using two strands of thread in the needle throughout, complete the first half of the border, beginning
in the marked centre. Complete the second half by
repeating the design, again stitching out from the
centre. If you work this way, the finished border
design will be symmetrically balanced out from the
centre, and you will have the same number of
unworked threads at each side.

APPLYING A BAND

Use this technique for decorating purchased towels.
Embroider the design on the evenweave band in
exactly the same way as for a prepared towel. Steam
press the embroidery on the wrong side, and then
make 12mm (½in) turnings all around, and baste.

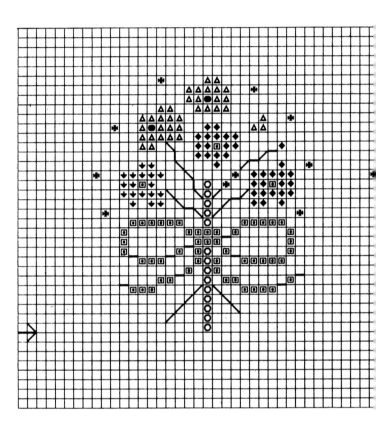

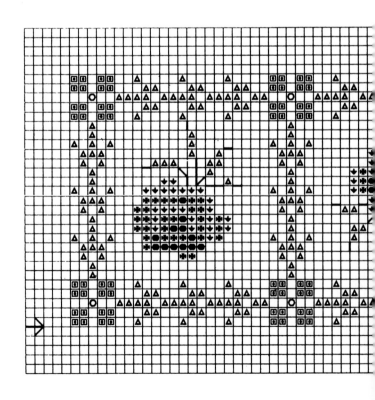

Pin and baste the band to the right side of the towel, 6cm (2½in) up from the lower edge. You may wish to insert a narrow lace edging between the band and the towel, to soften the edge. Machine stitch in place, using matching sewing thread. Remove the basting stitches and steam press to finish.

Centre

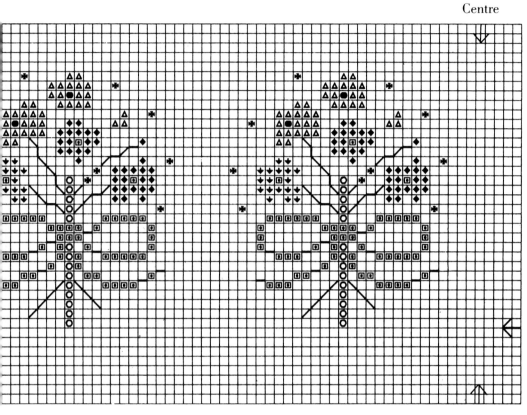

To complete each border, repeat the design working outwards from the centre.

Centre

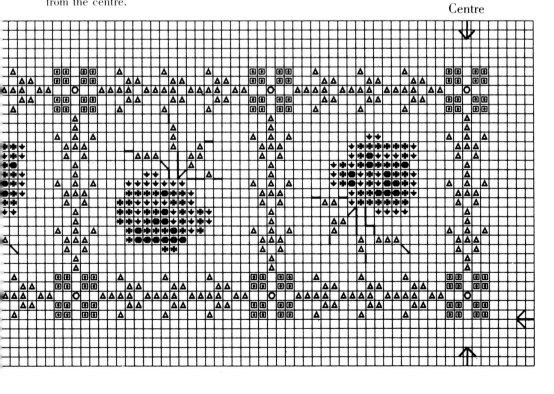

Drinks Tray

Based on the old rhyme 'Boys and girls come out to play, the moon doth shine as bright as day', this attractive oval drinks tray would make a lovely present for a Christmas or birthday, or perhaps to mark a special occasion, such as retirement.

If this cheerful picture seems wasted when destined to be half hidden under cups or mugs, you might prefer to set it into an oval picture frame, perhaps opting for a coloured background fabric.

COME OUT TO PLAY ▲

- ⬛ white (bks 926)
- ÷ 832 gold
- ↑ 225 flesh (bks 3354)
- ✳ 3354 pink

- ● 3350 deep pink
- = 598 blue (bks 926)
- ◆ 733 olive
- ↓ 731 dark olive
- � 422 buff

- ⊡ 831 brown
- I 926 grey blue
- ◣ 924 dark grey blue
- ○ 3024 light grey (bks 535)
- △ 535 dark grey

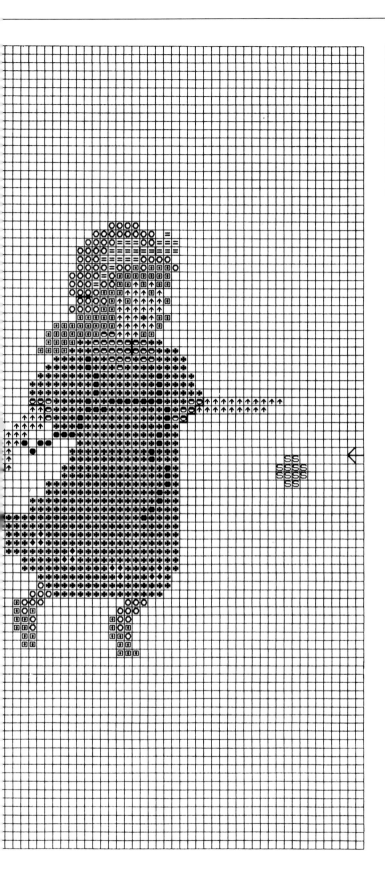

DRINKS TRAY

YOU WILL NEED

For a tray measuring 33cm × 20.5cm
(13in × 8in) with a 28.5cm × 16cm
(11¼in × 6¼in) oval cut out:

*40cm × 30cm (16in × 12in) of cream evenweave
(Aida) fabric, 14 threads to 2.5cm (1in)
DMC stranded embroidery cotton in the colours
given in the panel shown opposite
No24 tapestry needle
33cm × 20.5cm (13in × 8in) of lightweight
iron-on interfacing
Oval wooden tray (for suppliers, see page 160)*

•

THE EMBROIDERY

Begin by stretching the prepared fabric in an embroidery frame (see page 7). Then, following the colour key and chart, complete the cross stitching, using two strands of thread in the needle throughout. Remove the embroidery from the frame and, if necessary, steam press it on the wrong side. Do not remove the basting stitches at this stage.

ASSEMBLING THE TRAY

Using a soft pencil, mark the mounting card (supplied with the tray) both ways along the centre.

Lay the embroidery face down on a clean surface. Centre the card over it, with the pencil lines and basting stitches matching, and lightly draw around the card outline, using the pencil. Remove the basting threads, carefully cut out the embroidery, and back it with the lightweight iron-on interfacing. Alternatively, trim the fabric to leave a 4cm (1½in) allowance, and run a gathering thread around 12mm (½in) away from the pencil line. Position the card and pull up the gathers evenly. Either lace across the back or secure the edges with masking tape.

Follow the manufacturer's instructions to complete the assembly of your tray.

Trim Bookmarks

Here are bookmarks to please any reader. Each has a motif delicately edged with lace and a ribbon rosette or with loop stitch and a fine cotton tassel.

Relatively quick and simple to make, any of these would make a cheering and thoughtful present for a bedridden or chair-bound invalid, and a welcome change from fruit or flowers.

Two of the designs are embroidered on specially purchased bookmarks, while the central marker, featuring the two magpies, is stitched on a handmade example.

Bookmarks inevitably take a considerable amount of wear and handling, and can become rather grubby, so it might be a good idea to protect your finished embroidery by spraying with a proprietory dirt repellant.

TRIM BOOKMARKS

YOU WILL NEED

For the *Mary's Canary* and *The Ten o'clock Scholar* bookmarks, each measuring about 25cm (10in) long:

One cream and one white prepared lace-edged bookmark, 18 threads to 2.5cm (1in), each bookmark 5cm (2in) wide (for suppliers, see page 160)
DMC stranded embroidery cotton in the colours given in the appropriate panel
No26 tapestry needle

For the *Magpie, Magpie* bookmark, also about 25cm (10in) long:

23cm (9in) of white evenweave prepared braid, 5cm (2in) wide, 15 threads to 2.5cm (1in)
DMC stranded embroidery cotton in the colours given in the appropriate panels
No24 tapestry needle
Matching sewing thread

•

THE EMBROIDERY

Working in an embroidery hoop (see page 6 for the instructions on how to stretch small pieces of fabric in a frame) and with basted centre lines, complete the embroidery, using two strands of thread in the needle throughout.

Remove the basting stitches and, if needed, steam press on the wrong side.

FINISHING THE MAGPIE BOOKMARK

Make a small double turning on the top edge and, with matching thread, hem in place.

To make a point on the lower edge, fold the bookmark lengthways in half with the wrong side facing out and backstitch the short edges together. Trim the corner, press the seam open and turn to the right side. Flatten out the bookmark, thus creating a point. Press on the wrong side, and slipstitch to hold.

Make the tassel by winding ordinary white basting thread around a piece of card about 3cm (1¼in) wide. Thread the end into a needle, slip off the tassel threads and bind the loose thread several times around the bunch, close to the top. Pass the needle up through the binding so that it comes out at the top of the tassel – ready to be sewn to the point.

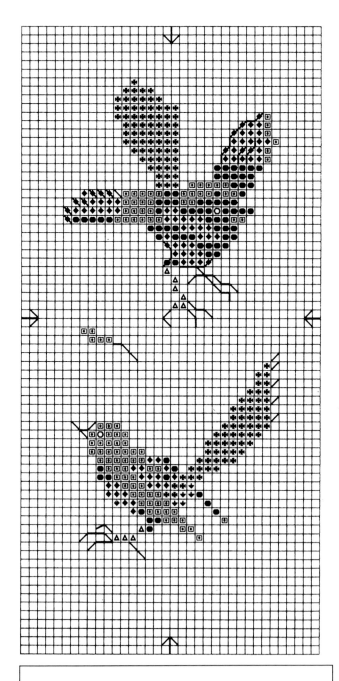

MAGPIE, MAGPIE ▲	⊡ 312 blue
	● 823 dark blue
◆ white (bks wings 312, body 823)	△ 3052 olive (bks feet)
	↓ 937 green
○ 472 gold	✱ 904 dark green

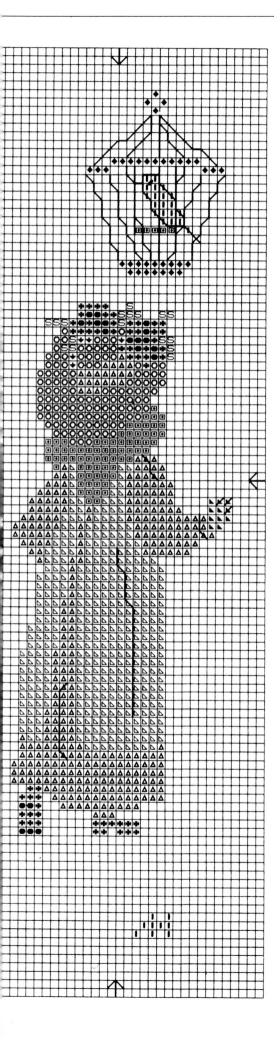

MARY'S CANARY ◄

- ◣ 948 flesh (bks 3326)
- | 445 pale yellow
- ◹ 727 yellow (bks 833)
- ↓ 783 orange
- ○ 833 ochre
- ✤ 3326 pink
- ● 335 deep pink
- △ 794 blue (bks 988)
- ⌇ 913 green
- ◆ 988 dark green
- ⊡ 3011 dark brown

TEN O'CLOCK SCHOLAR ►

- ◣ white (and bks 415*)
- | 948 flesh
- ✤ 778 pink (bks 3766)
- ○ 3766 sea green (bks 931)
- ● 931 deep blue green
- ◆ 738 straw
- ↓ 435 brown
- △ 612 drab brown
- ⊡ 611 dark brown

Note: one additional backstitch colour*

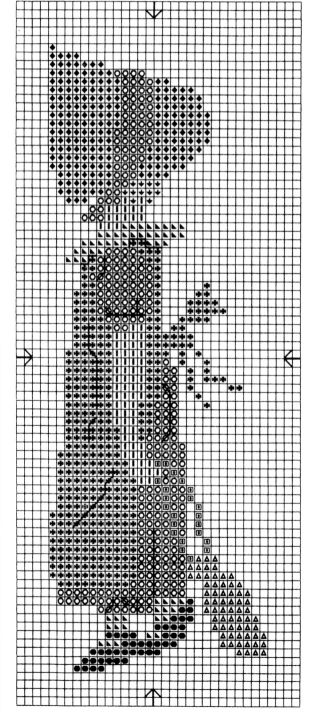

GIFTS FOR BABIES *and* CHILDREN

A cross stitch project makes a thoughtful gift for a new baby or small child. This chapter includes gift ideas such as small, hand-sized toys for a new-born baby or baby's christening, as well as a doll's bed quilt and a chair-cover that would delight any child.

Baby Hand-Toys

Nursery animals, just big enough for small hands to hold, are embroidered on one side only in colourful cross stitch patterns.

These easy-to-sew shapes are gently padded to give roundness and softness, and when a toy is not being held by baby, it can be hung at the side of the crib by its ribbon loop.

BABY HAND-TOYS

YOU WILL NEED

For three Hand-toys, each measuring
approximately 13cm × 9cm (5in × 3½in):

Six 18cm × 13cm (7¼in × 5in) rectangles of
white Hardanger, 22 threads to 2.5cm (1in);
two pieces for each toy
DMC stranded embroidery cotton in the colours
given in the panels
Sufficient loose synthetic filling for each toy
90cm (1yd) of white satin ribbon, 6mm (¼in) wide
No26 tapestry needle
Matching sewing thread
Three 15cm × 10cm (6in × 4in) pieces of
cardboard (use a breakfast cereal box, or
similar packaging)
Tracing paper

THE EMBROIDERY

All three toys are embroidered and made up in the
same way. For each toy, prepare one of the two
pieces of evenweave fabric and stretch it in a frame
(see page 7). Following the appropriate chart,
complete the cross stitching, using two strands of
thread in the needle throughout, and working one
cross stitch over two threads of ground fabric.
Steam press on the wrong side, if needed.

MAKING UP THE TOYS

Trace the outline of the appropriate toy; transfer
it to the cardboard, marking the position of the
arrows. Cut out the template; centre it on the wrong
side of the embroidery, matching the edges of the
cross stitching and aligning the arrows. Draw round
the shape with a pencil.

Working freehand, draw a second (cutting) line
6mm (¼in) beyond the first pencil (stitching) line.
Do not cut out the toy shape at this stage; the fabric
tends to fray during sewing, and it is therefore best
to complete the stitching first.

Cut the ribbon into three equal lengths; set two
aside for the remaining toys, and fold one length in
half. Place the back and embroidered front fabrics
right sides together. With the cut ends of the ribbon
protruding just beyond the raw edges of the fabric,
lay the folded ribbon between the two sections, as
marked on the chart.

With the ribbon inside, pin and baste the
sections together, stitching between the two marked
lines. Using matching sewing thread, either
machine stitch or backstitch around the edge,
sewing on the seamline and leaving a small opening
for the filling, as indicated on the chart.

Cut out, following the outer pencil line. Snip into
any curves, taking care not to cut the seam.
Remove the basting stitches and turn the toy
through to the right side. Steam press, and then
finger press the seam flat.

Gently fill the toy, using a knitting needle to
push small amounts of the filling into awkward
shapes, such as the cat's ears. Turn in the edges of
the opening and slipstitch to close.

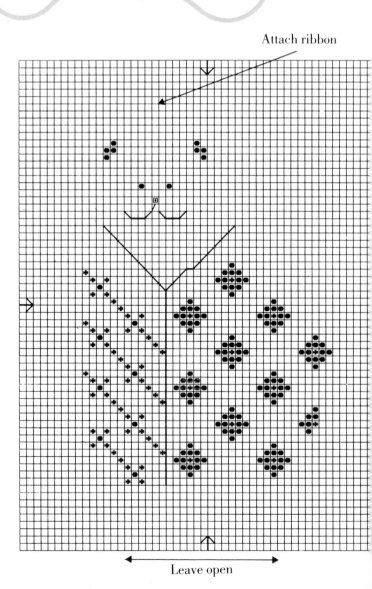

Attach ribbon

Leave open

Attach ribbon

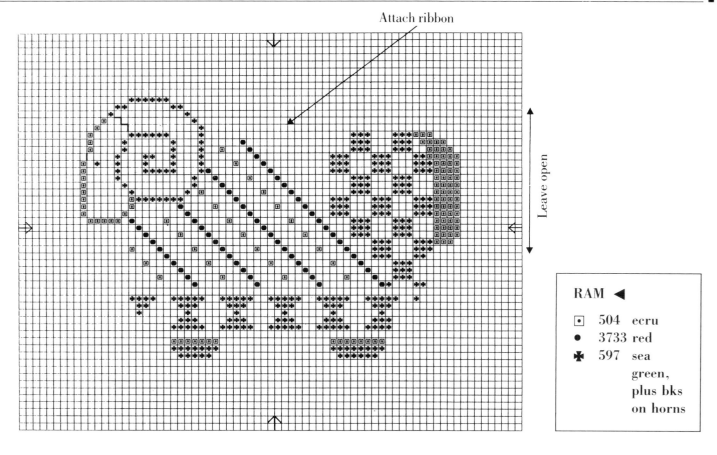

Leave open

RAM ◄

⊡	504	ecru
●	3733	red
✳	597	sea green, plus bks on horns

TEDDY ►

⊡	744	yellow
●	833	ochre, plus bks nose and mouth
✳	581	olive green, plus bks shirt and trousers

CAT ◄

✳	3705	red
●	334	light blue
⊡	798	deep blue, plus bks mouth and body

Attach ribbon

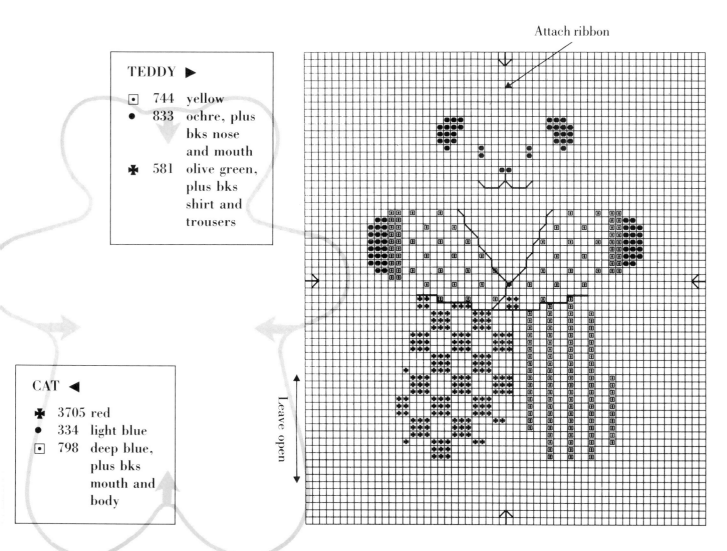

Leave open

Teddy Bear Companions

The story of the Three Bears is the perfect choice for decorating a cushion and padded back for a child's chair. The ingenious tie-on back incorporates a deep pocket, sufficiently large to hold a child's favourite possessions, including several cuddly toys.

If you wish to economize on the evenweave fabric, you could make the cushion back and the back pocket of the tie-on back from plain or patterned furnishing or other heavyweight cotton. Note, however, that the padded front portion is made from one piece, folded over.

TEDDY BEAR COMPANIONS

YOU WILL NEED

For a chair-back measuring 23cm × 20cm (9in × 8in), and a chair cushion measuring 23cm (9in) square, excluding the frills, which are 4cm (1½in) wide:

60cm (²/₃yd) of pale khaki evenweave Aida fabric, 110cm (43in) wide, 16 threads to 2.5cm (1in)
30cm (12in) of matching cotton sateen, 90cm (36in) wide, for the frills
120cm (1¹/₃yd) of contrasting seam binding, 12mm (½in) wide
24cm × 23cm (9½in × 9in) of medium-weight synthetic batting
DMC stranded embroidery cotton in the colours given in the panels
No26 tapestry needle
25cm (10in) square cushion pad

PREPARING THE FABRIC

Following the cutting layout, cut out the chair-back and the cushion sections from evenweave fabric. Seam allowances are included in the measurements given in the diagram.

Cut the sateen fabric into three strips across, each measuring 10cm (4in) deep, and put these to one side.

THE EMBROIDERY

Both the chair-back and the cushion are embroidered in the same way. With the fabric prepared and stretched in a frame (see page 7), centre lines basted in both directions and position line marked for the chair-back design (Back 2), begin the cross stitching.

Working with two strands of thread in the needle and following the appropriate chart, complete the embroidery. Work the backstitching last of all and note that a single strand is used for the lines on the rush seat of the chair-back design. Remove the finished embroidery from the frame and steam press it on the wrong side.

CUTTING LAYOUT

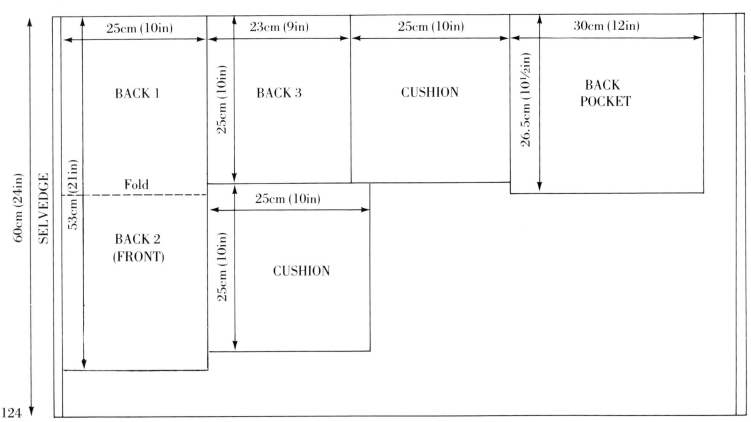

MAKING UP THE CHAIR-BACK

Using the basting lines as a guide, trim the fabric to measure 48.5cm × 23cm (19in × 9in), making sure the embroidered motif stays in the centre of the front section.

To make the frill, cut two 50cm (20in) lengths of sateen. Fold each piece lengthwise in half, right sides together, and machine stitch along the short edges. Turn through and press. Run a gathering thread along the bottom edge of each frill and pull up to measure 23cm (9in). With the right side facing, baste the frill to each long side of the front section raw edges just inside the seam allowance. Machine stitch in place.

For the ties, cut the seam binding into four equal lengths. Baste to the two short edges as shown in the diagram, so that the binding lies on the right side of the fabric and will be attached as the seams are sewn.

Place the batting on the wrong side of the lining section (Back 3), with the raw edges of three sides matching, and pin and baste it in position. Fold a single 12mm (½in) turning, enclosing the batting, at the remaining (chair top) edge of the back lining,

and baste. With right sides together and the folded edge at the top (centre foldline), place the lining on the embroidered section. Stitch along the side and bottom edges. Trim the batting back and trim across the corners, then turn right side out and machine close to the fold along the top edge, stitching through all layers.

On the pocket section, machine stitch a double 12mm (½in) turning on one long edge. Make a pleat 2cm (¾in) deep at each side of the bottom edge, 6cm (2½in) in from the outer edge, and baste across.

On the main section, snip into the seam allowance on the foldline. Place the pocket section with the right side facing the wrong side of Back 1. Baste and machine stitch around three sides, leaving the top unstitched. Trim the corners and turn through to the right side. Machine stitch across the corners of the pocket top to strengthen.

MAKING UP THE CUSHION

To make the frill, join together the remaining lengths of sateen along the short edges to give a total length of 186cm (63in). Machine stitch the two

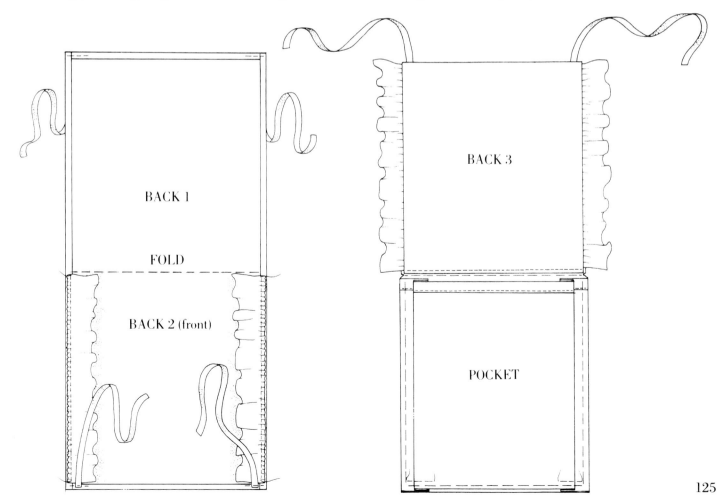

BACK 1

FOLD

BACK 2 (front)

BACK 3

POCKET

short edges together to form a circle, then turn through to the right side and press the seam open.

Fold the circular piece lengthwise in half, with wrong sides together, and press the fold. Run a gathering thread through both thicknesses along the lower edge and pull up the gathers to fit. Pin and baste to the right side of the cushion front, and stitch as for the chair-back.

Place the backing fabric and the embroidery right sides together, then baste and machine stitch around, leaving a 15cm (6in) opening in the middle of one side. Trim across the corners and turn through to the right side. Remove the basting threads and lightly press. Insert the cushion pad and slipstitch the opening to close.

To protect the finished embroidery from scuff marks and other accidents, it would be a good idea to spray it with a proprietory dirt repellant.

CUSHION ▼

	white	◁	783 deep gold		807 turquoise	⊡	435 light brown
⊖	3047 cream	◆	224 pale pink	÷	598 blue		(bks 3781)
⊆	676 pale yellow	●	3733 pink	↓	523 drab green	○	611 brown (bks 3781)
	(bks claws)	◣	504 pale turquoise		(bks on tablecloth)	✼	3781 dark brown
			(bks 733)	△	733 green	=	453 grey

CHAIR-BACK ▲

	white	◆	224 pale pink	✱	435 light brown
S	3047 cream (bks 783)	⊡	3733 pink (bks 504)		(horizontal bks on
I	676 pale yellow	◣	504 pale turquoise		chair front)
△	783 deep gold (bks 3781)	✦	598 blue (bks 435)	●	3781 dark brown

Patchwork Quilt

Cross stitched in a single colour and in a relatively large stitch, this doll's cradle quilt is simple to make – so simple that, with a little adult guidance, a young girl could easily embroider the design.
This is based on a traditional American patchwork pattern called Martha Washington's Star.

PATCHWORK QUILT

YOU WILL NEED

For a Doll's cradle quilt, measuring
41cm × 25cm (16in × 10in):

*46cm × 30cm (18in × 12in) of white linen,
20 threads to 2.5cm (1in)
43.5cm × 27.5cm (17in × 11in) of white linen,
finer than the above, or cotton backing fabric
43.5cm × 27.5cm (17in × 11in) of lightweight
synthetic batting
3 skeins of red 666 DMC stranded
embroidery cotton
No18 tapestry needle
Matching sewing thread*

•

THE EMBROIDERY

Stretch the prepared fabric in a frame (see page 7). Using three strands of thread in the needle and working one cross stitch over two threads of fabric, follow the chart to complete one half of the embroidery. Repeat, embroidering the second half as instructed on the chart.

When stitching, bear in mind that with very openweave fabrics it is better not to strand the embroidery thread from one area to another, since the thread will show through on the right side. Trim any long threads, and steam press the finished embroidery on the wrong side.

COMBINING THE LAYERS

Trim the top fabric to measure 43.5cm × 27.5cm (17in × 11in), and place it face down. Centre the batting on top and then lay the backing fabric over the batting, smoothing all layers as you go. Pin and baste the three layers together, stitching outward from the centre. In this way, by smoothing the fabrics out towards the edges, you will avoid unsightly puckering in the middle of the quilt. Baste horizontally, vertically and diagonally both ways. Baste from the centre outwards; leave a long tail at the centre and work out to one corner, then rethread the needle and work out to the other corner, avoiding knots at the centre.

TYING THE QUILT

Working on the right side, and using either matching sewing thread or quilting thread if you prefer, make a single stitch in the centre of each square that depicts a cross. Bring the needle out to the right side, leaving an 8cm (3in) tail underneath; make a tiny stitch in the centre of the cross, and return the needle to the wrong side. Make a second stitch at the same point. On the wrong side, tie the ends together – right over left, left over right – but do not pull too tightly. Trim the ends of the knot. Complete, tying all knots in this way.

FINISHING THE EDGES

Trim the batting by 12mm (½in) all around the edge. Turn under the seam allowances of the top and backing, bringing that of the top over the edge of the batting. Baste and then, using matching thread, slipstitch around the edges. For a traditional finish, hand quilt around the edge, setting the first row two threads in from the edge and the second row eight threads in, just clear of the embroidered border.

Remove the basting threads and lightly steam press if necessary.

HAND QUILTING

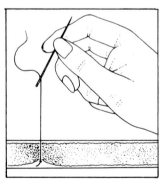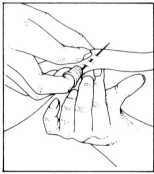

1 Working in a hoop will keep your fabric evenly stretched and give a pleasant puffed effect to the finished quilting. Using a quilting needle and a fairly short length of quilting thread, knot the end. Pull the knot through the backing fabric and into the batting.

2 With a thimble on the second finger of the sewing hand, make several stitches. Keep your

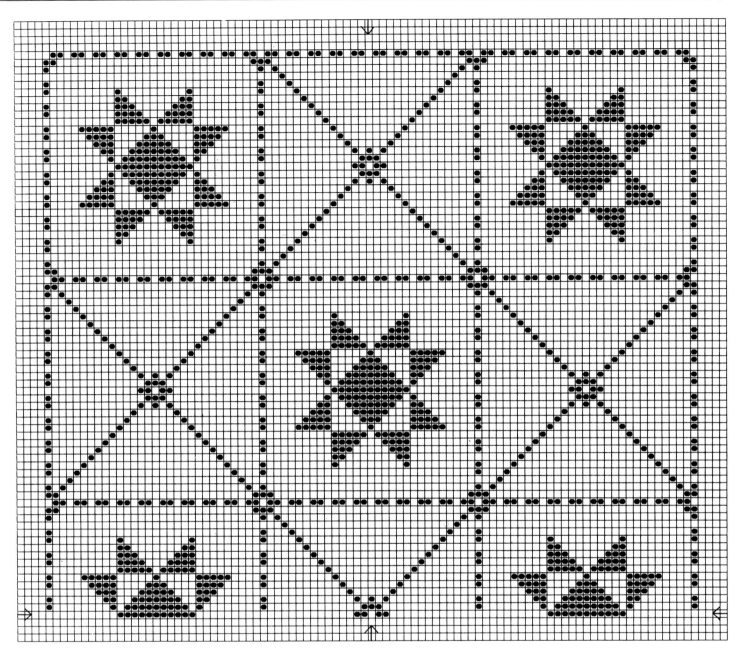

thumb pressed down on the fabric, just ahead of the
needle, while the hand below, also with a thimble
on the first or second finger, feels the needle and
guides it back through the layers.

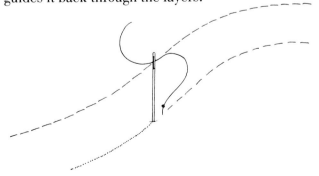

3 Finish off with a couple of back stitches or make
a knot close to the last stitch and take the thread
through to the back. Pull the knot through into the
batting and cut the thread.

PATCHWORK QUILT ▲
● 666 red

Complete the second half of the design by embroidering
in reverse from the centre line.

Scatter Cushions

Make this charming set of tiny cushions to scatter on a young teenager's bed, or mix them with other cushions to fill an armchair or sofa. The scale of these cushions is small, but you could easily increase the size by adding a border of velvet, in a dark matching shade, effectively framing the centres.

SCATTER CUSHIONS

YOU WILL NEED

For three cushion covers, each measuring
24cm (9½in) square:

*58cm × 29cm (23in × 11½in) each of cream,
pink and grey evenweave Aida fabric,
14 threads to 2.5cm (1in)
100cm (40in) each of gold (metallic), grey and red
fabric-covered piping
DMC stranded embroidery cotton in the colours
given in the appropriate panel
No24 tapestry needle
Matching sewing threads
Three 25cm (10in) square cushion pads
Tracing paper*

•

THE EMBROIDERY

All three cushions are made in the same way. To
make one cushion, cut the evenweave fabric in half
to give two pieces, each measuring 29cm (11½in)
square. Following the instructions given on page
7, prepare and stretch one of the pieces of fabric
in an embroidery frame.

Referring to the appropriate chart, and colour
key, complete the cross stitching, using two strands
of thread in the needle throughout, and working the
backstitch details on top. Finish by backstitching
the outline around the design, working each quarter
section symmetrically, and again, using two strands
of the thread in the needle.

Remove the embroidery from the frame and
steam press on the wrong side.

MAKING UP THE CUSHION COVER

Trim the edges of the embroidery and the backing
section of evenweave so that they each measure
26.5cm (10½in) square. Following the outline of
the cushion corner given with the chart for the Pied
Piper, make a template from tracing paper, reversing each corner on the centre lines to complete the
cushion shape. Using the template, mark and then
cut around the curved corners on both sections of

evenweave fabric. A 12mm (½in) seam allowance
is included.

Metallic gold piping has been used for the
Rumplestiltskin design, red for the Pied Piper and
grey for The Goosegirl. Lay the piping on the right
side of the embroidery, placing the raw edge just
inside the seam allowance. Baste, and then use the
piping foot to machine stitch it in place (see page
8). Overlap the two ends, neatly angling the raw
edges into the seam allowance. If the piping can be
spliced (unlike purchased metallic varieties), this
would give an invisible join.

With right sides of the cushion front and back
together, baste and machine stitch around the
edges, leaving a 16cm (6¼in) opening in the
middle of one side, again using the piping foot, and
stitching as close as possible to the piping.

Remove the basting threads, snip into the
corners and turn the cover to the right side. Before
inserting the cushion pad, give the corners a
slightly rounded shape by tucking in the point of
each corner by about 12mm (½in). Finger-press
the resultant rounded shaping for about 4cm (1½in)
on each side of the point, gently easing the curve
into the side seams at each corner. Loosely overcast
the seam to hold the shape. Insert the cushion pad,
turn in the opening and slipstitch to close, using
matching sewing thread.

PIED PIPER ▶

↑	725	yellow
◤	741	amber
I	370	ochre (bks 317)
S	3779	flesh (bks 927)
✳	606	red (bks 317)
⊡	309	magenta (bks 317)
◺	703	green
O	943	veridian green (bks 317)
●	3052	drab green
◆	927	light grey (bks 317)
↓	317	grey (rat's feet; bks 927)
△	413	dark grey (all whiskers and piper's moustache)

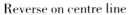

Reverse on centre line

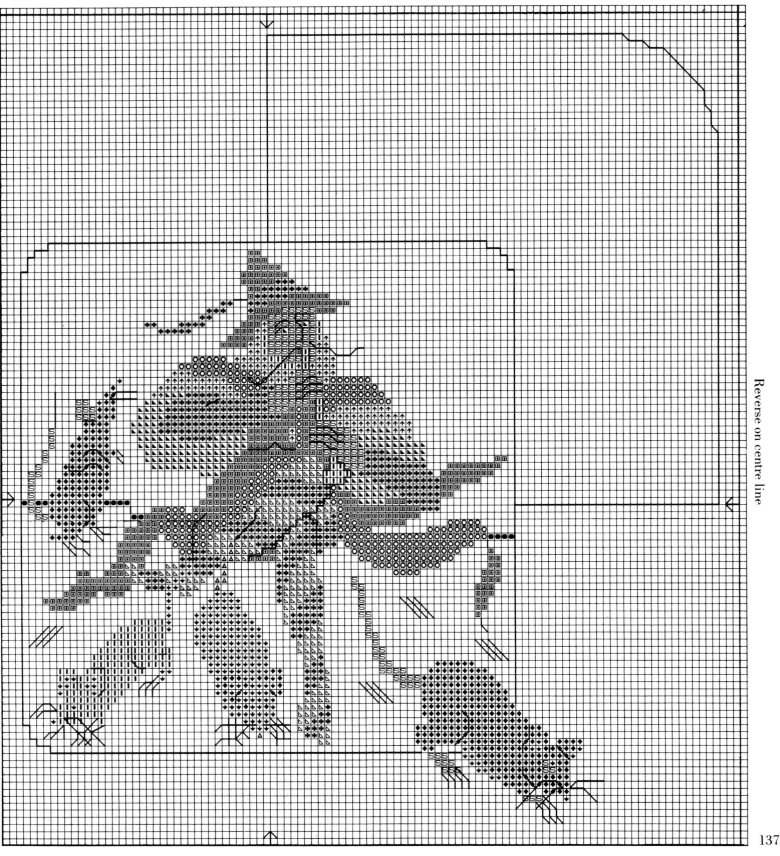

Reverse on centre line

137

THE PIED PIPER

The Pied Piper put his brass flute to his lips and began to play a
sad, haunting melody. Suddenly, the streets of Hamelin seethed
with rats; the Pied Piper walked towards the river and sat down,
whereupon the rats threw themselves into the icy water and
disappeared forever.

THE GOOSEGIRL

The princess, tricked by her servant into minding geese, speaks to the head of her horse Falada. Every morning, as she sets out to tend her flock of geese, she stops at the gateway and says, 'Alas, dear Falada, there you hang.' And Falada answers, 'Alas, Queen's daughter, there you go, if your mother knew your fate, her heart would break with grief so great.' Then she goes on her way till she comes to the common, where she sits down and begins to comb out her hair.

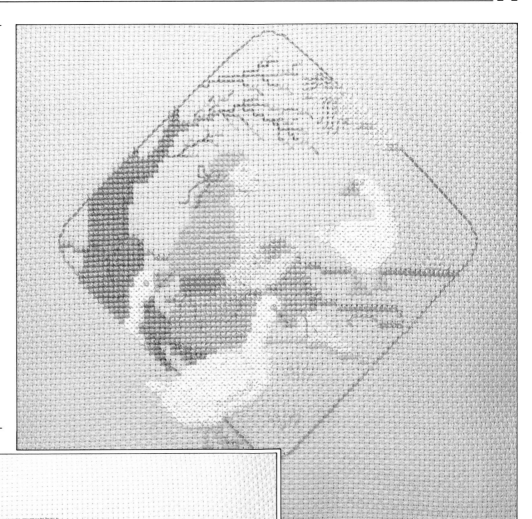

RUMPLESTILTSKIN

Appearing suddenly, as if from nowhere, the rather eccentric and diminutive little man asked the miller's daughter, 'What will you give me if I spin the straw into gold?' 'The ring from my finger', she replied. Rumplestiltskin hopped onto the stool and began to spin. In just a few minutes he had changed the pile of straw into a hundred bobbins of pure gold thread.

RUMPLESTILTSKIN ▲

S 834 corn (and bks stems)

✦ 725 yellow (bks 3045)

○ gold thread (and thread being spun; bks 3045)

◆ 3779 flesh (bks 3011)

● 3712 red (bks 3766)

◣ 3753 pale turquoise (bks 3766)

⊡ 3766 turquoise (bks 3347)

| 3347 green

△ 3045 light brown (bks 3011)

✤ 3011 brown (bks 3045)

THE GOOSEGIRL ▼

- `=` white (bks 3072)
- ◆ 725 yellow (bks 3013)
- ↑ 834 gold (bks 725)
- | 948 flesh (bks 3706; bks eye 927)
- ● 3354 dusky pink (bks outline around design)
- ◁ 3706 deep pink (bks hair ribbon)
- ○ 927 drab turquoise (bks 3354)
- ◠ 772 pale green (bks grass)
- ↓ 3013 olive green
- ⊡ 3052 drab green (bks tree branches)
- △ 3072 grey (bks 927 on sleeve; bks 926 on horse)
- ✳ 926 dark grey

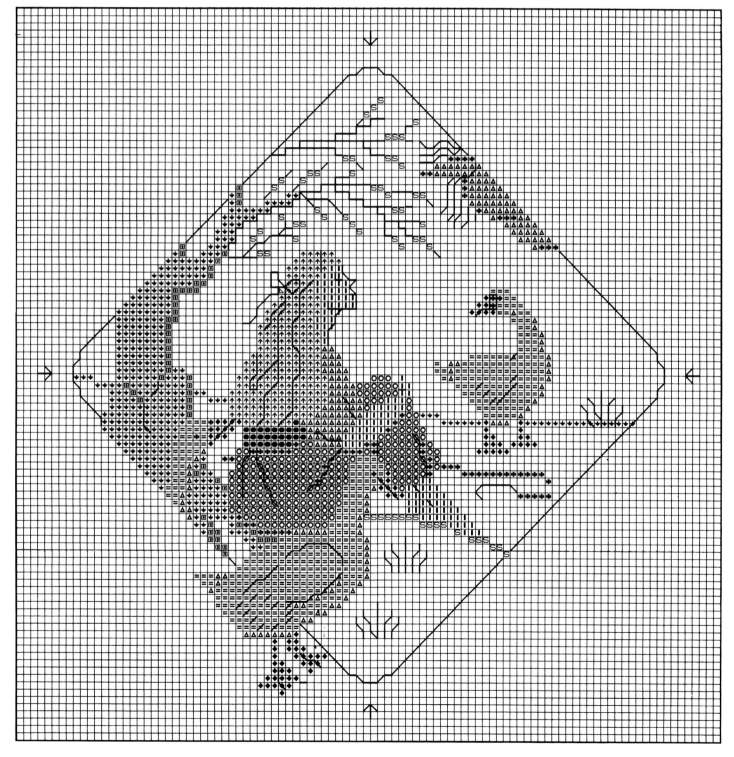

With Love and Kisses

What better way to send a special greeting than with a card you've made yourself? Choose doves and hearts to celebrate a new baby's arrival or christening, jolly Santa Claus for Christmas, or two colourful parrots for a toddler's second birthday.
Each motif is easily stitched, and displayed in a press-together card mount which couldn't be quicker or simpler to use.

WITH LOVE
AND KISSES

YOU WILL NEED

For the Christening card, measuring overall
20cm × 14.5cm (8in × 5¾in), with a rectangular
portrait cut out, 14cm × 9.5cm (5½in × 3¼in):

*23cm × 18cm (9in × 7¼in) of pale pink linen,
28 threads to 2.5cm (1in)
DMC stranded embroidery cotton in the colours
given in the appropriate panel
No26 tapestry needle
Best Wishes greetings card mount (for suppliers,
see page 160)*

For the Santa Claus christmas greetings card,
measuring overall 14cm × 9cm (5½in × 3½in),
with an oval cut out, 9cm × 7cm (3½in × 2¾in):

*17cm × 13cm (6¾in × 5in) of pale green linen,
28 threads to 2.5cm (1in)
DMC stranded embroidery cotton in the colours
given in the appropriate panel
No26 tapestry needle
Christmas card mount (for suppliers, see page 160)*

For the Second birthday card, measuring overall
20cm × 14.5cm (8in × 5¾in), with a rectangular
portrait cut out, 14cm × 9.5cm (5½in × 3¾in):

*23cm × 18cm (9in × 7¼in) of white evenweave
Aida fabric, 18 thread to 2.5cm (1in)
DMC stranded embroidery cotton in the colours
given in the appropriate panel
No26 tapestry needle
Birthday greetings card mount (for suppliers,
see page 160)*

●

THE EMBROIDERY

Prepare the fabric and mount it in a small hoop,
following the instructions on page 6. When
embroidering greetings cards, it is important to
avoid too much overstitching on the back of the
fabric in order to prevent unsightly lumps showing
on the right side. For the Santa Claus and Christen-

ing designs, work one cross stitch over two threads
of fabric throughout.

Referring to the appropriate chart and colour
key, complete the cross stitching, using two strands
of thread in the needle for all three designs. You
will find it easier to embroider Santa's beard if you
stitch the pale grey shadows first, and then fill in
with white. Similarly, complete the motif first on
the cradle of the Christening design before filling
in with white. Steam press the embroidery on the
wrong side.

CHRISTENING CARD ▼		
I white	⊡ 734	green (and bks border)
✸ silver, plus bks around doves	○ 828	pale blue
◆ 725 ochre	△ 3072	pale grey
● 957 pink		

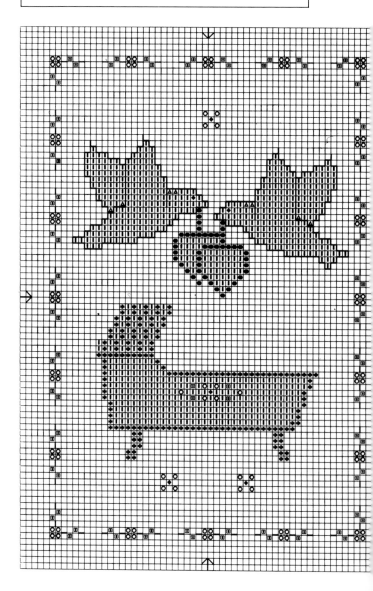

If you leave the basting stitches in at this stage, you will find them useful in helping to centre your design on the card.

ASSEMBLING THE CARDS

Open out the three sections of the card. Trim the embroidery until it is about 12mm (½in) larger than the marked area around the cut-out window. Using the basting stitches as a guide, centre the motif over the cut-out area – measuring an equal distance at each side of the basting – and press in place.

Remove the basting stitches. Fold over the left-hand section of the card and press to cover the embroidery, giving a neat permanent seal to your special greetings card.

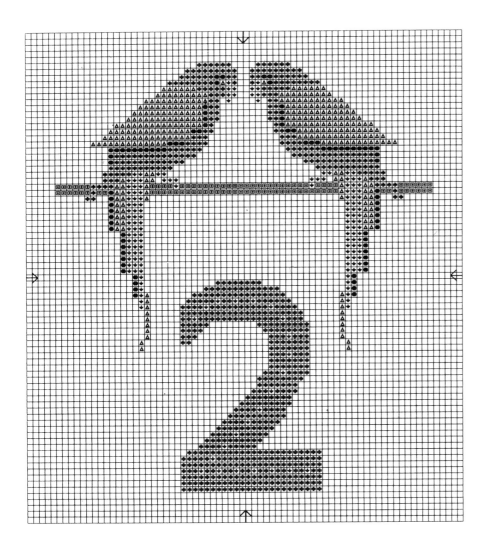

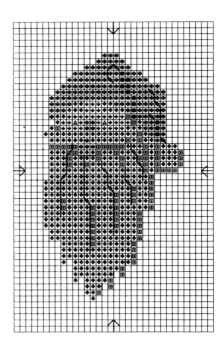

SANTA CLAUS ▲

- ◆   white
- ↓   754 flesh
- ✳   606 red
- ●   347 dark red (and bks hat)
- △   518 blue
- ⊡   3072 pale grey (and bks beard)

SECOND BIRTHDAY ▲

- ↓   725 yellow
- ✳   351 red
- △   704 green
- ⊡   734 olive green
- ●   798 blue

Frilled Baby Basket

This pretty and practical basket, designed to hold all baby's odds and ends, would delight any new mother. The tie-on washable cover can easily be removed for laundering – and when baby grows up you can always use the basket for toys or for family shopping.

The cover is designed for a basket with a top measuring approximately 29cm × 42cm (11½in × 16½in), but the size can easily be adjusted.

The design could also be adapted to a Moses basket, but in this case, having measured the basket and made an allowance for the baby's head, it would be best to cut the fabric straight across at the head end, and take the frill around the sides and bottom only.

You could also cut the back and batting in one piece and omit the ties, so that the top will fit snugly around the baby.

FRILLED
BABY-BASKET COVER

YOU WILL NEED

For a cover measuring approximately
33cm × 46cm (13in × 18in) across, including a
3cm (1¼in) frill all around:

*33cm × 46cm (13in × 18in) of white evenweave
Linda fabric, or linen, 16 threads to 2.5cm (1in)
33cm × 46cm (13in × 18in) of white cotton lawn
for the lining
28cm × 40cm (11in × 16in) of medium-weight
synthetic batting
160cm (1¾yd) of white pre-gathered broderie
anglaise edging, 4cm (1½in) wide
140cm (1½yd) of white taffeta ribbon,
2.5cm (1in) wide
DMC stranded embroidery cotton in the colours
given in the panels
Matching sewing threads
Baby basket of your choice
Tracing paper*

•

PREPARING THE FABRIC

First, enlarge the graph pattern on to tracing paper (see page 8); mark the positioning lines for the embroidery, and cut out.

Baste the centre of the embroidery fabric both ways; place the paper pattern on the straight grain, matching the centre lines, and baste around the curved edge. Repeat on the opposite side. Mark the positioning lines for the two motifs, as shown on the graph pattern.

Using the paper pattern, cut out the batting and the lining fabric, adding a 12mm (½in) seam allowance all around on the lining pieces, and around the curved edge only on the batting sections.

THE EMBROIDERY

With the prepared fabric stretched in a hoop, begin the embroidery. Following the charts given opposite, and working with two strands of thread in the needle, complete the cross stitching. Finish by working the backstitch details, using a single strand of thread.

Steam press on the wrong side. Cut out, adding a 12mm (½in) seam allowance all round.

MAKING THE COVER

Working on the right side, baste the lace edging around the outer edge of the embroidered section, with the raw edge placed just inside the seam allowance, and leaving a 3cm (1¼in) space in the middle of both long sides. This will allow the cover to fit snugly around the basket handle, and the two sides to be lifted independantly. Turn under the short edges of the frill twice to neaten.

With the embroidery and the two lining sections right sides together, place the batting on top. Baste and machine stitch around the outer edge. Trim the batting close to the seam, clip into the curves and turn the cover through to the right side. Turn under the two straight edges of the lining, unpicking a few stiches of the outer seam as necessary, then baste and machine stitch across.

Cut the ribbon in half and attach to each side, stitching the centre of the ribbon over the seam allowance in the space left, to neaten. Remove all basting threads and lightly press to finish.

BABY-BASKET COVER
1 SQUARE = 2.5cm (1in)

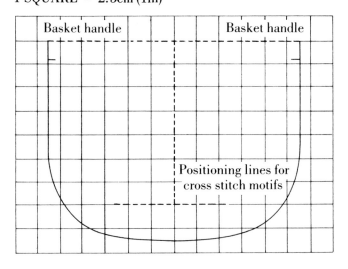

CUT TWO FROM BATTING
CUT TWO FROM LINING
Reverse on centre line and cut
one for cover top

◀ SWALLOW

- ◆ 3047 cream
- ◣ 3078 pale yellow
  (bks 725)
- ↓ 725 yellow (bks 798)
- ○ 745 flesh (eyes 798,
  mouth 350)
- ⊡ 602 deep pink (bks 336)
- ✱ 350 vermilion
- I 798 pale blue (bks 824)
- △ 824 blue
- ● 336 dark blue

BUTTERFLY ▶

- ○ 3078 pale yellow
  (bks inner
  veins 725)
- ◆ 725 yellow
  (bks 350)
- ⊡ 602 deep pink
- ✱ 350 vermilion
- ↓ 3747 pale blue
- ● 824 blue
  (bks antennae)
- △ 676 deep buff
  (bks 350)

Miniature Pictures

What better way to build up a pretty collection of pictures than to embroider them yourself?

Taken from three nursery rhymes – 'Little maid, pretty maid, whither goest thou?', 'Rock-a-bye, baby, on the tree top', and 'A little girl quite well and hearty', any of these small pictures would make a lovely gift for a child and – who knows? – might perhaps encourage the child to take up embroidery herself.

If you decide to embroider all three designs, it would obviously be preferable to use the same background colour for each. The little girl and the sleeping baby would both look attractive against the blue background.

If you prefer to keep to a cream fabric, it might be a good idea to backstitch in grey around the mob cap and along the edge of the apron where the white would meet the cream.

QUITE WELL, QUITE HEARTY ▼

- ○ 963 pink (bks 335, initial M 3041)
- ⊡ 335 deep pink (bks 3041)
- ↓ 948 flesh
- ✳ 3041 purple (bks 3011)
- I 966 green
- ◆ 3052 sap green
- ◣ 307 yellow (eye 833)
- △ 833 ochre (bks cage, bird's legs)
- ● 3011 dark brown

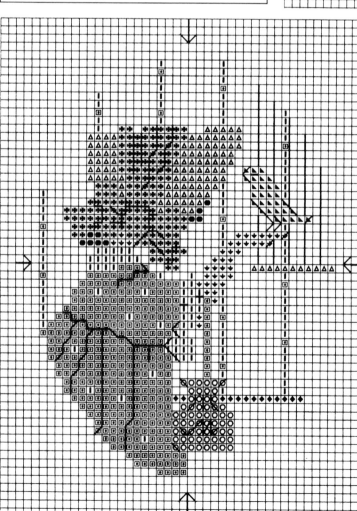

LITTLE MAID ◀

↑ white (and bks 318*)

◣ 948 flesh (bks 352)

○ 352 pink

◺ 800 blue

● 823 navy blue

△ 312 dark blue

⊡ 436 light brown (bks 434)

✚ 434 brown

◆ 415 pale grey

↓ 648 grey

Note: one additional backstitch colour*

ROCK-A-BYE BABY ▼

= white

↑ 726 yellow

I 676 gold

◣ 754 flesh
   (bks eye 3688)

△ 3688 pink

● 602 deep pink

◺ 3756 pale blue
   green (bks 519)

⊡ 519 blue green

⊂ 955 pale green

↓ 913 green (bks twigs)

◆ 951 fawn

✚ 3011 brown

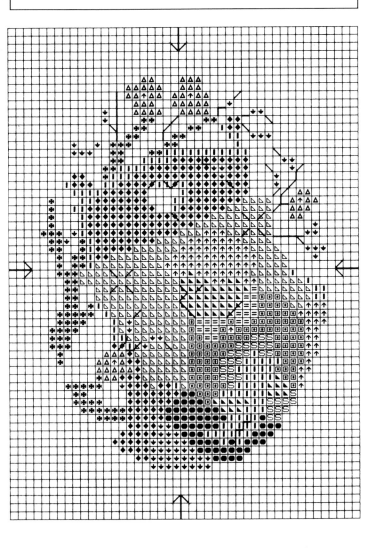

MINIATURE PICTURES

YOU WILL NEED

For the *Little Maid* picture, measuring
18cm × 13cm (7¼in × 5in):

*23cm × 18cm (9in × 7¼in) of blue evenweave
(Aida) fabric, 18 threads to 2.5cm (1in)
DMC stranded embroidery cotton in the colours
given in the appropriate panel
No 26 tapestry needle
Oval brass frame (for suppliers, see page 160)*

For *Quite Well, Quite Hearty,* and
Rock-a-Bye Baby miniatures, each measuring
11.5cm × 9cm (4½in × 3½in):

*28cm × 18cm (11in × 7¼in) of white evenweave
linen, 26 threads to 2.5 cm (1in)
DMC stranded embroidery cotton in the colours
given in the appropriate panels
No 26 tapestry needle
Two oval brass frames (for suppliers, see page 160)*

•

THE EMBROIDERY

Each picture is worked in the following way. With
the prepared fabric stretched in a hoop and the
centre marked both ways (see page 6) you are
ready to begin the cross stitching. Use two strands
of thread in the needle throughout, except for the
backstitching of Little Maid, which is worked in a
single strand. When working a fairly openweave
fabric, such as the linen used here, bear in mind
that threads should not be stranded across an open
area or they will be seen from the right side.

Remove the fabric from the frame and steam
press on the wrong side, if necessary.

MAKING UP THE PICTURES

Follow the manufacturer's instructions for
assembling the pictures, checking that you have
allowed sufficient fabric to fill the frame before
cutting out by fitting the paper template supplied
into the frame.

Tied-on Pillow Cover

Dress up a plain yellow pillow with this pretty tied-on cover, embroidered on crisp white evenweave cotton. The idea is practical as well as pretty, for the embroidered cover can easily be removed at night-time, to cut down on laundering.

The little boy blue of the nursery rhyme, incidentally, is an allusion to Cardinal Wolsey, who neglected his flock in his attempts to engineer the divorce of Henry VIII.

TIED-ON
PILLOW COVER

YOU WILL NEED

For a pillow cover measuring 46cm × 35cm
(18in × 14in):

*48.5cm × 38cm (19in × 15in) of white evenweave
(Aida) fabric, 14 threads to 2.5cm (1in)*
*48.5cm × 38cm (19in × 15in) of white backing
fabric, either fine cotton or linen*
*250cm (2⅔yds) of cornflower blue satin ribbon,
2cm (¾in) wide*
140cm (1½yds) of cornflower blue bias binding
*DMC stranded embroidery cotton in the colours
given in the panel*
No24 tapestry needle
Matching sewing thread

•

THE EMBROIDERY

With the prepared fabric stretched in a frame (see
page 7) baste the positioning lines for the motif,
following the chart given opposite.

Using two strands of thread in the needle
throughout, work all the cross stitching first and
then the backstitching.

Take out the basting stitches; remove the fabric
from the frame, and steam press on the wrong side.

MAKING UP THE PILLOW COVER

With right sides together, baste the top
and backing fabric along the two long edges.
Machine stitch, taking 12mm (½in) seams. Press
the seams open.

For the ties, cut the ribbon into eight equal
lengths. With the wrong side facing, baste them
in pairs to each of the short edges, placing
them 10cm (4in) in from the corners (see the
diagram below).

Cover the short edges with bias binding, at the
same time enclosing the ribbon ends. Overlap the
raw edges of the binding at the seams. Press and
turn through to the right side. Slip the cover over
a contrast pillow and tie in place.

LITTLE BOY BLUE ▶

◹ white (bks 341)
⊆ 744 yellow (bks 738)
↓ 738 corn
◆ 834 deep yellow
| 3779 flesh (bks 3712)
△ 3712 red (bks 3052)
○ 341 blue (bks 792)
● 792 dark blue (bks eye;
    bks 3011)
✶ 3052 olive
⊡ 3011 brown

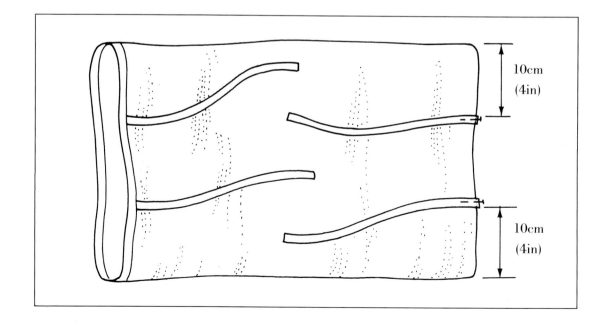

10cm
(4in)

10cm
(4in)

INDEX

CONVERSION CHART

Not all of these colour conversions are exact matches,
but the closest substitutes have been given in every case.

DMC	ANCHOR	MADEIRA	DMC	ANCHOR	MADEIRA	DMC	ANCHOR	MADEIRA	DMC	ANCHOR	MADEIRA
White	1	White	520	269	1514	776	24	0503	959	186	1113
223	895	0812	523	859	1512	778	968	0808	961	40	0610
224	893	0813	535	401	1809	781	308	2213	962	52	0609
225	892	0814	550	101	0714	783	307	2211	963	23	0608
300	352	2304	563	204	1207	792	177	0905	966	206	1209
301	349	2306	564	203	1208	793	121	0906	972	303	0107
307	289	0104	581	280	1609	794	120	0907	975	355	2305
309	42	0507	597	168	1110	798	155	0911	976	309	2302
310	403	Black	598	928	1111	799	130	0910	988	257	1402
311	148	1006	600	65	0704	800	153	0907	989	256	1401
312	979	1011	601	78	0703	807	168	1108	992	187	1202
317	235	1714	602	63	0702	814	44	0514	993	186	1201
318	399	1802	603	62	0701	817	47	0211	3011	856	1607
319	246	1313	604	55	0614	818	48	0502	3012	854	1606
321	42	0510	605	50	0613	822	390	1908	3013	854	2110
322	978	1004	606	335	0209	823	150	1008	3024	391	1901
326	59	0508	611	898	2107	824	164	1010	3041	871	0806
334	161	1003	612	832	2108	826	161	1012	3045	888	2103
335	42	0506	613	831	2109	828	158	1101	3046	887	2206
336	150	1007	640	392	1905	830	906	2114	3047	852	2205
340	118	0902	644	830	1907	831	906	2201	3051	846	1508
341	117	0901	648	900	1813	832	907	2202	3052	860	1509
347	19	0407	666	46	0210	833	907	2202	3053	859	1510
349	13	0212	676	891	2208	834	874	2204	3072	900	1805
350	11	0213	677	886	2207	839	380	1913	3078	292	0102
351	10	0214	680	901	2210	842	376	1910	3325	159	1002
352	9	0303	702	226	1306	869	944	2105	3326	26	0504
355	5968	0401	703	237	1307	891	35	0411	3328	11	0408
367	262	1312	704	256	1308	892	28	0412	3345	268	1406
368	261	1310	712	387	2101	893	27	0413	3347	267	1408
370	888	2112	718	88	0707	899	27	0505	3348	265	1409
372	88	2210	721	324	0308	900	326	0208	3350	69	0603
413	401	1713	722	323	0307	904	258	1413	3354	75	0608
414	400	1801	725	306	0113	907	255	1410	3364	843	1603
415	398	1802	726	295	0109	911	205	1214	3609	85	0710
422	373	2102	727	293	0110	912	209	1212	3688	970	0605
433	371	2008	729	890	2209	913	921	1711	3705	35	0410
434	310	2009	730	924	1614	915	70	0705	3706	33	0409
435	365	2010	731	281	1613	924	851	1706	3712	10	0406
436	363	2011	732	281	1612	926	850	1707	3713	23	0502
444	291	0108	733	281	1611	927	849	1708	3731	76	0603
445	288	0103	734	279	1610	928	900	1709	3733	75	0408
451	815	1808	738	942	2013	930	922	1712	3747	120	0901
452	232	1807	741	304	0201	931	781	1711	3750	170	1006
453	231	1806	742	303	0114	932	920	1002	3752	159	1002
469	267	1503	743	297	0113	935	862	1505	3753	975	1001
470	266	1502	744	301	0112	937	268	1504	3755	140	1013
471	280	1501	745	300	0111	943	188	1203	3756	158	1001
472	253	1414	747	158	1104	945	881	2313	3761	159	1014
500	879	1705	754	4146	0305	948	778	0306	3766	167	1105
503	876	1702	758	868	0403	951	880	2308	3772	379	2312
504	213	1701	761	8	0404	955	202	1210	3779	4146	2313
518	169	1106	762	397	1804	957	52	0612	3781	905	2006
519	168	1105	772	264	1604	958	187	1114	3799	152	1713

SUPPLIERS

The following mail order company has supplied some of the basic items needed for making up the projects in this book:

Framecraft Miniatures Limited
148-150 High Street
Aston
Birmingham, B6 4US
England
Telephone (021) 359 4442

Addresses for Framecraft suppliers worldwide
Ireland Needlecraft Pty. Ltd.
2-4 Keppel Drive
Hallam, Victoria 3803
Australia

Danish Art Needlework
PO Box 442, Lethbridge
Alberta T1J 3Z1
Canada

Sanyei Imports
PO Box 5, Hashima Shi
Gifu 501-62
Japan

The Embroidery Shop
286 Queen Street
Masterton
New Zealand

Anne Brinkley Designs Inc.
246 Walnut Street
Newton
Mass. 02160
USA

S A Threads and Cottons Ltd.
43 Somerset Road
Cape Town
South Africa

For information on your nearest stockist of embroidery cotton, contact the following:

DMC

UK
DMC Creative World Limited
62 Pullman Road
Wigston
Leicester, LE8 2DY
Telephone: 0533 811040

USA
The DMC Corporation
Port Kearney Bld.
10 South Kearney
N.J. 07032-0650
Telephone: 201 589 0606

AUSTRALIA
DMC Needlecraft Pty
P.O. Box 317
Earlswood 2206
NSW 2204
Telephone: 02599 3088

ANCHOR

UK
Kilncraigs Mill
Alloa
Clackmannanshire
Scotland, FK10 1EG
Telephone: 0259 723431

USA
Coats & Clark
P.O. Box 27067
Dept CO1
Greenville
SC 29616
Telephone: 803 234 0103

AUSTRALIA
Coats Patons Crafts
Thistle Street
Launceston
Tasmania 7250
Telephone: 00344 4222

MADEIRA

UK
Madeira Threads (UK) Limited
Thirsk Industrial Park
York Road, Thirsk
N. Yorkshire, YO7 3BX
Telephone: 0845 524880

U.S.A.
Madeira Marketing Limited
600 East 9th Street
Michigan City
IN 46360
Telephone: 219 873 1000

AUSTRALIA
Penguin Threads Pty Limited
25-27 Izett Street
Prahran
Victoria 3181
Telephone: 03529 4400

ACKNOWLEDGEMENTS

The author would like to offer her grateful thanks to the following people who helped with the cross stitching of projects in this book with such skill and enthusiasm: Gisela Banbury, Clarice Blakey, Caroline Davies, Christina Eustace, Janet Grey, Elizabeth Hall, Anne Whitbourn, and to Julie Hasler for her designs – Little Disaster page 16, A Frog He Would A-wooing Go page 50, Wee Willie Winkie page 96, Ten o'clock Scholar page 112 and Little Maid page 150.

The publishers would also like to thank The Monogrammed Linen Shop, 68 Walton Street, London SW3, and Thomas Goode and Co., 19 South Audley Street, London W1Y 6BN, for kindly supplying linen and china on page 50.
Thanks are also due to DMC Creative World Ltd. for providing the black and white charts.